2

English Grammar: Step by Step

Written by Elizabeth Weal
Illustrated by Anastasia Ionkin

Tenaya Press
Palo Alto, CA

For my students

©2010 Elizabeth Weal

All inquiries should be addressed to
Elizabeth Weal
Tenaya Press
3481 Janice Way
Palo Alto, CA 94303

650-494-3941
ElizabethWeal@tenaya.com
http://TenayaPress.Tenaya.com

Book design: Stuart Silberman
Cover: Beth Zonderman

About the cover

The cover is a photograph of a portion of a mola. Molas are part of the traditional dress of the Central American Cuna (or Kuna) tribe of the San Blas Islands, a chain of tropical islands along the Atlantic coast of Panama. Molas, which also can be found in Colombia, are handmade using a "reverse appliqué" technique. Several layers of different-colored cloth are sewn together; the design is then formed by cutting away parts of each layer.

Cover photo by Mary Bender.

ISBN 978-0-9796128-9-3

Contents

Welcome

A note to students

Welcome to *English Grammar: Step by Step 2*, a book that will help you understand the basics of English grammar so that you can speak and write English correctly.

The assumption behind this book is that anyone can learn English grammar, regardless of their level of education. To ensure that this occurs, grammar concepts are presented in a step-by-step fashion, starting at the most basic level. Each new concept is followed by exercises that give you the opportunity to practice what you've learned and additional exercises at the end of each chapter provide even more practice. All of the answers to the exercises are in an appendix, so you can check your work as you go. A dictionary of all the words used in this book is included in the back of the book, making it easy to look up words you don't know how to spell. The dictionary also includes pronunciation.

This book assumes that you have a very basic knowledge of English grammar. Specifically, you should know how to use the verbs *to be* (*am*, *is* and *are*) and *to have*; and how to use possessive adjectives (*his*, *her*, *our*, etc.). You also should know how to identify nouns, pronouns and adjectives and use basic punctuation (periods and question marks) correctly. If these topics are unfamiliar to you, work through *English Grammar: Step by Step 1*; then continue with this book.

Keep in mind that the focus of this book is exclusively on grammar. Learning English requires many other skills in addition to grammar, such as pronunciation, listening comprehension, vocabulary development, and so on. At the same time, if you want to advance in English you'll need a solid foundation in basic grammar, which is precisely what this book provides.

A note to teachers

English Grammar: Step by Step 2 was written to help Spanish-speaking students learn grammar in a simple, straightforward manner. It focuses on many of the grammar points that are most confusing to new English language learners: prepositions, simple present tense verbs and present progressive verbs. It assumes that students know how to use the verbs *to be* and *to have* and understand the use of possessive adjectives (*his*, *her*, *our*, etc.). Students also should be able to identify nouns, pronouns and adjectives. and use basic punctuation (periods and question marks) correctly. If students are not familiar with these topics, they should work through *English Grammar: Step by Step 1*; then continue with this book.

Teachers can use this book as a classroom text in classes with only Spanish-speakers or as a supplement for Spanish-speaking students in mixed-language classes. These books can also be made available to students in distance learning programs and in school bookstores that stock ESL materials. Many teachers also sell these books to students so they can use it at home.

Because the book is available in English and Spanish, teachers who don't speak Spanish can read the English version to learn some basic differences between English and Spanish grammar, then make the Spanish version of the book available to their students.

Acknowledgements

Many people gave me the encouragement I needed to embark on the second book in this series. My friend and colleague Maria Kleczewska was the inspiration for the first book and offered invaluable encouragement the second time around. Lorraine Reston provided valuable editorial input. Gabriela Urricariet was a skilled and thorough editor and translator. Her eye for detail helped make this book a success. Anastasia Ionkin, an incredibly talented artist, created the drawings that make this book fun to read. Stuart Silberman transformed my original manuscript from a sea of gray into a document that's both easy to use and inviting to read. Beth Zonderman designed the book cover. Julie Reis and Phyllis Mayberg were excellent copy editors. My friend Mary Bender opened my eyes to the beauty of Latin American textiles in general and to molas in particular. A mola from her collection is pictured on the cover of this book.

I also want to thank the many Sequoia Adult School staff members—including Barbara Hooper, Lionel De Maine, Pat Cocconi, Ana Escobar, Soledad Rios, Maria Ibarra, and Juan Ramirez—who have supported my efforts and helped make my books available to Sequoia Adult School students.

My extraordinary husband Bruce Hodge unflaggingly supported my efforts and helped with countless tasks, from design assistance to 24/7 technical support. Without his help, this book would not exist. My daughters Chelsea and Caroline provided editorial and artistic input. Finally, I want to thank the many students who completed my first book; then thanked me for making English grammar understandable. They continue to be my inspiration.

Chapter 1

My shoes are under the chair.

Imagine this situation: You're late for work. Your boss, who speaks only English, calls you on your cell phone to find out where you are. If you can't answer him, you're going to have a problem! In this chapter, you'll learn how to answer questions about where you are and also about where things are at home and on the job.

At the end of this chapter you will be able to
- identify prepositions.
- use prepositions to describe where people and objects are located.
- ask and answer questions about where people and objects are located.

A ***preposition*** is a word that shows the relationship between words in a sentence. En, a, entre and sin are all Spanish prepositions. A ***preposition of location*** or a preposition of place describes where something or someone is located, In this section, you'll learn several prepositions of location. In the following illustrations, each preposition of place is <u>underlined</u>.

The rabbit is <u>in</u> the box.	**The rabbit is <u>on</u> the box.**	**The rabbit is <u>above</u> the box.**	**The rabbit is <u>under</u> the box.**
(El conejo está en la caja. El conejo está dentro de la caja.)	(El conejo está en la caja. El conejo está sobre la caja.)	(El conejo está arriba de la caja.)	(El conejo está abajo de la caja.)

Note that **in** and **on** have different meanings. In general, **in** means dentro de and **on** means sobre.

A preposition is a part of speech

To understand English or Spanish grammar, it is very useful to understand *parts of speech*, names that you use to specify how a word is used in a sentence. Here is a summary of the parts of speech you should be familiar with.*

Part of speech	Definition	Examples
noun (*sustantivo*)	A person, place, animal or thing	**teacher** (maestra); **school** (escuela); **dog** (perro); **table** (mesa)
pronoun (*pronombre*)	A word that takes the place of a noun	**I** (yo); **you** (usted, tú, ustedes); **we** (nosotros, nosotras); **he** (él); **she** (ella)
adjective (*adjetivo*)	A word that modifies or describes a noun or pronoun	**big** (grande, grandes); **beautiful** (bonito, bonita, bonitos, bonitas)
verb (*verbo*)	A word that shows action or state of being	**is** (ser, estar); **have** (tener); **work** (trabajar)
preposition (*preposición*)	A word that shows the relationship between other words in a sentence.	**under** (abajo de); **above** (arriba de)

*If you are unclear how to identify nouns, pronouns, and adjectives, read *Gramática del inglés: Paso a paso 1*. We'll talk more about how to identify verbs in Chapter 4.)

1.1.a Directions: One of the three words in each group of words is <u>not</u> a preposition. Cross out the word that is <u>not</u> a preposition. (If you don't know a word, look it up in the dictionary in the back of this book.)

1. ~~boy~~, above, in
2. in, husband, on
3. television, under, above
4. on, above, tired

1.1.b Directions: One of the three words in each group of words is <u>not</u> a noun. Cross out the word that is <u>not</u> a noun. Remeber that a *noun* is a person, <u>place</u>, animal or thing.

1. microwave, ~~beautiful~~, house
2. apartment, table, in
3. eggs, book, happy
4. black, dress, house
5. cousin, aunt, at
6. cat, dog, dirty
7. above, coffee, car
8. year, month, are

1.1.c Directions: One of the three words in each group of words is <u>not</u> a pronoun. Cross out the word that is <u>not</u> a pronoun. Remember that a *pronoun* is a word that can replace a noun.

1. he, ~~doctor~~, she
2. white, she, it
3. I, store, you
4. ball, it, they
5. they, we, pencil
6. backpack, it, you
7. she, sad, we
8. happy, he, they

1.1.d Directions: One of the three words in each group of words is <u>not</u> an adjective. Cross out the word that is <u>not</u> an adjective. Remember that an *adjective* is a word that describes a noun or pronoun.

1. ~~cashier~~, tired, handsome
2. blue, airplane, purple
3. yellow, happy, it
4. sad, lazy, person
5. beautiful, apple, red
6. old, new, dog
7. above, heavy, thin
8. interesting, good, student

1.1.e Directions: Write the preposition that describes each drawing.

1. The rabbit is __on____ the box.
2. The rabbit is _____ the box.
3. The rabbit is _____ the box.
4. The rabbit is _____ the box.

You'll often use *prepositions of location* to tell where things are located around your house. The following illustrations show the rooms in a house and what's often found in each one. The dictionary in the back of this book tells you how these words are pronounced. You'll use these words in the exercises on the next page.

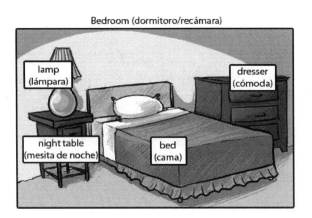

Kitchen (cocina)

microwave (microondas)
blender (licuadora)
counter (encimera)
refrigerator (refrigerador)
kitchen sink (fregadero)
stove (cocina, estufa)

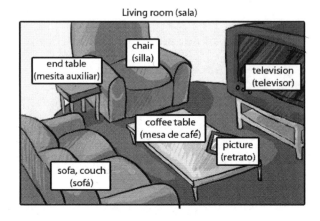

Living room (sala)

chair (silla)
end table (mesita auxiliar)
television (televisor)
coffee table (mesa de café)
picture (retrato)
sofa, couch (sofá)

Bedroom (dormitoro/recámara)

lamp (lámpara)
dresser (cómoda)
night table (mesita de noche)
bed (cama)

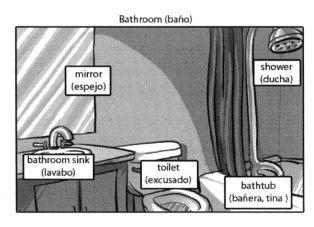

Bathroom (baño)

mirror (espejo)
shower (ducha)
bathroom sink (lavabo)
toilet (excusado)
bathtub (bañera, tina)

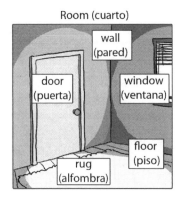

Room (cuarto)

wall (pared)
door (puerta)
window (ventana)
floor (piso)
rug (alfombra)

You use the preposition **in** to refer to objects in a room. For example:

► The apples are <u>in</u> the kitchen. (Las manzanas están en la cocina.)

► The toys are <u>in</u> the living room. (Los juguetes están en la sala.)

1.2.a Directions: Identify the items in each picture.

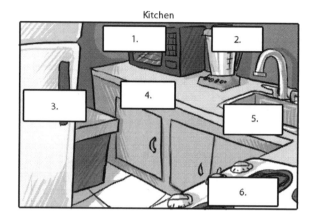

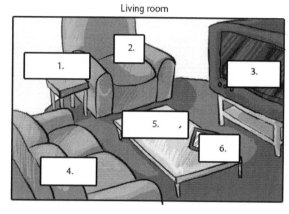

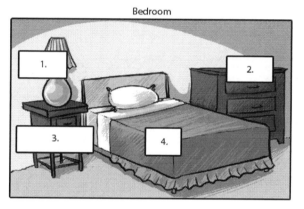

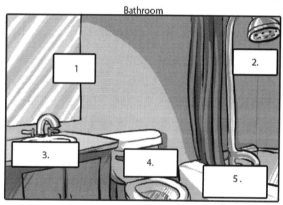

Kitchen

1. microwave
2. _____
3. _____
4. _____
5. _____
6. _____

Living room

1. _____
2. _____
3. _____
4. _____
5. _____
6. _____

Bedroom

1. _____
2. _____
3. _____
4. _____

Bathroom

1. _____
2. _____
3. _____
4. _____
5. _____

Here are a few more prepositions of location to study.

The rabbit is between the boxes. (El conejo está entre las cajas.)	**The rabbit is next to the box.** (El conejo está al lado de la caja.)	**The rabbit is in front of the box.** (El conejo está delante de la caja.)	**The rabbit is behind the box.** (El conejo está detrás de la caja.)

The preposition between

In both English and Spanish, the preposition **between** (entre) is always followed by two singular nouns or by one plural noun. For example, if a cat is between two boxes, you say

▶ The cat is <u>between</u> the boxes. (El gato está entre las cajas.)

If the cat is between a box and a ball, you say

▶ The cat is <u>between</u> the box and the ball. (El gato está entre la caja y la pelota.)

It is incorrect to say

▶ The cat is ~~between the box~~. (El gato está ~~entre la caja~~.)

Prepositions composed of more than one word

You may have noticed that several prepositions in both English and Spanish are more than one word long. These are sometimes called **_compound prepositions_**. For example, **next to** is two words; **al lado de** is three words. Regardless of the language, what's important is to include every word of the compound preposition and to make sure you properly separate the words that comprise the compound preposition. Thus, you say

▶ The cat is next to the box. (El gato está al lado de la caja.)

It is incorrect to say

▶ The cat is ~~next the box~~. / The cat is ~~nexto the box~~.

1.3.a Directions: Write the preposition that describes each drawing.

1.   2.   3.   4.

1. The rabbit is ___behind___ the box.   3. The rabbit is _____ the box.

2. The rabbit is _____ the boxes.   4. The rabbit is _____ the box.

1.3.b Directions: One of the sentences in each pair is not a correct sentence. Cross out the incorrect sentence.

1a. The table is in front of the sofa.   1b. ~~The table is in the sofa.~~

2a. The couch is between the end tables.   2b. The couch is between the end table.

3a. I am in the bedroom.   3b. I am on the bedroom.

4a. The blender is in the counter.   4b. The blender is on the counter.

5a. She is next to her sister.   5b. She is next her sister.

6a. I am in front my apartment.   6b. I am in front of my apartment.

7a. The pencil is on the floor.   7b. The pencil is in the floor.

8a. The store is between the school.   8b. The store is between the school and the park.

9a. Your shoes are next the window.   9b. Your shoes are next to the window.

10a. The oranges are in the kitchen.   10b. The oranges are on the kitchen.

1.3.c Directions: Translate these sentences.

1. Los libros están al lado de la lámpara.   The books are next to the lamp.

2. El cuadro está arriba del sofá. _____

3. Mi casa está al lado de la tienda. _____

4. Mi tía está en la cocina. _____

5. Tu libro está entre el cuaderno y el bolígrafo. _____

6. Las sillas están delante de la mesa. _____

7. Nuestro carro está delante de la casa. _____

Now that you know some prepositions, you're ready to start asking questions about where things are. Study this conversation.

Note the following:

► The mother uses **Where is** in the first question because she is asking her daughter about her backpack, which is singular.
► The mother uses **Where are** in the second question because she is asking her daughter about her shoes, which are plural.

Note that the response to the first question is

► It is on the floor. (Está en el piso.)

It is less common, but also correct, to reply

► My backpack is on the floor. (Mi mochila está en el piso.)

Questions made with **where** (dónde) and the verb **to be** have this form:

Question word and verb		Rest of the sentence	Translation
Where	is	the book?	¿Dónde está el libro?
Where's		the book?	¿Dónde está el libro?
Where	are	the books?	¿Dónde están los libros?

Contractions

A *contraction* is a word that is made by joining two words. You can use a contraction to shorten **where is** to **where's**. As you can see from the chart above, the following questions mean the same thing:

► Where's the book? Where is the book?

You cannot use a contraction to shorten **where are**. For example, you cannot ask,

► ~~Where're~~ the books?

1.4.a Directions: Look at the pictures. Then, answer the questions using one of the following prepositions: **in**, **on**, **under**, **between**, **in front of** or **next to**. Note that each line represents one word in the

1. The shoes are ___under___ the table.

2. The sock (*calcetín*) is _____ the shoes.

3. The dog is _____ the floor.

4. The bread (*pan*) is _____ the table.

5. The cheese (*queso*) is _____ _____ the bread.

6. The ball is _____ _____ _____ the dog.

7. The broom (*escoba*) is _____ _____ _____ the table.

8. The dog is _____ the living room.

1.4.b Directions: Write a *Where question* before each answer. Don't forget to end each question with a question mark (**?**).

1. ___Where is the ball?___   The ball is on the floor.

2. _____ The books are on the table.

3. _____ The towels (*toallas*) are in the bathroom.

4. _____ The socks are on the dresser.

5. _____ The pizza is in the kitchen.

6. _____ The students are at the park.

In this section, you'll learn to ask questions to find out where people are. Read this conversation between a husband and wife speaking on their cell phones.

Note the following:

► In the first conversation the wife uses the preposition in because she's referring to a room, kitchen.

► In the second conversation she uses the preposition at because she's referring to a place in the community.

The table below tells you which prepositions to use when you're specifying locations.

Preposition	Example in English	Example in Spanish
Use **at** before the name of a place	<u>at</u> the library <u>at</u> the beach <u>at</u> the restaurant <u>at</u> the park <u>at</u> home <u>at</u> work <u>at</u> school <u>at</u> church <u>at</u> Rick's Restaurant <u>at</u> Hoover Park	en la biblioteca en la playa en el restaurante en el parque en casa en el trabajo en la escuela en la iglesia en el restaurante Rick's en el parque Hoover
Use **at** for a street address	<u>at</u> 313 Grove Street	en el 313 de la calle Grove
Use **in** before a room, city, state or country	<u>in</u> the kitchen <u>in</u> the office <u>in</u> the classroom <u>in</u> San Francisco <u>in</u> California <u>in</u> Mexico <u>in</u> the United States	en la cocina en la oficina en el aula, en la clase en San Francisco en California en México en los Estados Unidos
Use **on** for a street name	<u>on</u> Ross Street	en la calle Ross

Notice the following:

► You never use **the** before the name of a specific place, such as **Rick's Restauran**t or **Hoover Park**. You do use **the** when you are referring to a general location such as **the restaurant** or **the park.**

► There is no good explanation for why you use **the** before the names of some places and not others. In general, you use **the** before general place names with the exception of **home**, **work**, **school** and **church**.

1.5.a Directions: Complete each sentence using **at, in** or **on**.

1. I am ___in___ the bedroom.
2. Laura is _____ home.
3. Jose is _____ New Orleans.
4. The teacher is _____ the classroom.
5. The party is _____ 17 Post Avenue.
6. Carlos is _____ the beach.
7. My sisters are _____ school.
8. Sam is _____ work.

9. Luis is _____ the United States.
10. Carlos is not _____ Chicago.
11. My uncles are _____ Mexico.
12. My house is _____ 222 Pine St.
13. My house is _____ Center Street.
14. Andrew is not _____ the bedroom.
15. Jose is a cook _____ Nick's Restaurant.
16. We are not _____ the park.

1.5.b Directions: One of the sentences in each pair is not a correct sentence. Cross out the incorrect sentence.

1a. Lisa is at the beach.
2a. Marian is in work.
3a. Maria is in the home.
4a. Our teacher is in the classroom.
5a. I am in the living room.
6a. The book is in the sofa.
7a. My parents are at the work.
8a. My friends are at Pedros Pizza Restaurant.
9a. Her house is on 8th Ave.
10a. I am no at work.
11a. The students are at the El Pueblo Market.
12a. We are at the beach.

1b. ~~Lisa is in the beach.~~
2b. Marian is at work.
3b. Maria is at home.
4b. Our teacher is at the classroom.
5b. I am at the living room.
6b. The book is on the sofa.
7b. My parents are at work.
8b. My friends are at the Pedros Pizza Restaurant.
9b. Her house is in 8th Ave.
10b. I am not at work.
11b. The students are at El Pueblo Market.
12b. We are in the beach.

1.5.c Directions: Translate these sentences.

1. Estoy en Chicago.   I am in Chicago.
2. Él está en Perú.
3. Juana es de Perú.
4. Mis amigos están en la playa.
5. Los estudiantes están en la biblioteca.
6. Tus libros están en la cama.
7. Los jugu tes están en el piso.

Chapter 1 Summary

Prepositions

A *preposition* is a word that shows the relationship between words in a sentence. En, a, entre and sin are all Spanish prepositions. A *preposition of location* describes where something or someone is located. The following are some common prepositions of location:

in	on	above
under	next to	between
in front of	behind/in back of	

Prepositions of location

The table below tells you which prepositions to use when you're specifying locations.

Preposition	Example in English	Example in Spanish
Use **at** before the name of a place	<u>at</u> the library <u>at</u> the beach <u>at</u> the restaurant <u>at</u> the park <u>at</u> home <u>at</u> work <u>at</u> school <u>at</u> church <u>at</u> Rick's Restaurant <u>at</u> Hoover Park	en la biblioteca en la playa en el restaurante en el parque en casa en el trabajo en la escuela en la iglesia en el restaurante Rick's en el parque Hoover
Use **at** for a street address	<u>at</u> 313 Grove Street	en el 313 de la calle Grove
Use **in** before a room, city, state or country	<u>in</u> the kitchen <u>in</u> the office <u>in</u> the classroom <u>in</u> San Francisco <u>in</u> California <u>in</u> Mexico <u>in</u> the United States	en la cocina en la oficina en el aula, en la clase en San Francisco en California en México en los Estados Unidos
Use **on** for a street name	<u>on</u> Ross Road	en la calle Ross

Where questions

Questions made with **where** (dónde) and the verb **to be** have this form:

Question word	Verb	Rest of the sentence	Translation
Where	is	the book?	¿Dónde está el libro?
Where	are	the books?	¿Dónde están los libros?

✏️ More Practice!

P1.a Directions: One of the three words in each group of words is <u>not</u> a preposition. Cross out the word that is <u>not</u> a preposition.

1. ~~boy~~, above, in
2. in front of, bed, between
3. she, at, next to
4. under, tired, behind

5. in front of, green, between
6. on, tall, next to
7. above, they, behind
8. across from, happy, under

P1.b Directions: One of the three words in each group of words is <u>not</u> a noun. Cross out the word that is <u>not</u> a noun.

1. book, ~~beautiful~~, student
2. shower, nurse, in
3. school, dog, bad
4. apartment, new, car

5. floor, is, bed
6. kitchen, sofa, dirty
7. above, sink, teacher
8. we, pencil, New York

P1.c Directions: One of the three words in each group of words is <u>not</u> a pronoun. Cross out the word that is <u>not</u> a pronoun.

1. she, ~~nurse~~, I
2. kitchen, it, they
3. I, window, she
4. they, you, hot

5. he, I, pencil
6. sick, they, you
7. school, I, she
8. picture, you, we

P1.d Directions: One of the three words in each group of words is <u>not</u> an adjective. Cross out the word that is <u>not</u> an adjective.

1. ~~dresser~~, red, new
2. sick, rabbit, purple
3. on, happy, green
4. aunt, expensive, healthy

5. beautiful, ugly, children
6. under, handsome, dirty
7. above, tall, thin
8. lazy, hardworking, study

P1.e Directions: One of the sentences in each pair is <u>not</u> a correct sentence. Cross out the incorrect sentence.

1a. ~~The books are next the lamp.~~
2a. The students are in the classroom.
3a. Yvonne is at home.
4a. The photos are in front the table.
5a. I am at work.
6a. The dog is between the chairs.
7a. My wife is at Berkeley Adult School.
8a. Susan is at the Benny's Restaurant.

1b. The books are next to the lamp.
2b. The students are on the classroom.
3b. Yvonne is in the home.
4b. The photos are in front of the table.
5b. I am at the work.
6b. The dog is between the chair.
7b. My wife is at the Berkeley Adult School.
8b. Susan is at Benny's Restaurant.

P1.f Directions: Write the preposition that describes each drawing.

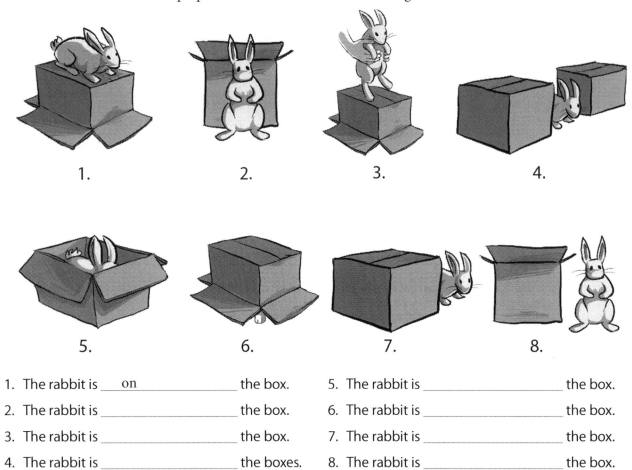

1.   2.   3.   4.

5.   6.   7.   8.

1. The rabbit is ___on___ the box.
2. The rabbit is _____ the box.
3. The rabbit is _____ the box.
4. The rabbit is _____ the boxes.

5. The rabbit is _____ the box.
6. The rabbit is _____ the box.
7. The rabbit is _____ the box.
8. The rabbit is _____ the box.

P1.g Directions: Complete each sentence using **at**, **in**, **on** or **between**.

1. I am ___in___ Chicago.
2. Adam is _____ Michoacan.
3. Jose is _____ work.
4. We are not _____ home.
5. The women are _____ church.
6. Caroline is _____ the beach.
7. The students are _____ the library.
8. Sam is not _____ work.

9. Luis is _____ the United States.
10. Carlos is not _____ Texas.
11. Your books are _____ the floor.
12. The photo is _____ the wall.
13. The plates are _____ the table.
14. My house is not _____ Redwood City.
15. Jose is _____ Nick's Pizza.
16. The boys are _____ Mitchell Park.

P1.h Directions: Translate the following sentences.

1. Tus llaves están en la mesa.   ___Your keys are on the table.___

2. Mi mochila está en la cocina.   _____

3. Samuel está en la iglesia.   _____

4. Los estudiantes están en la biblioteca.   _____

5. Tus libros están al lado de la lámpara.   _____

P1.i Directions: Read the paragraph and answer the questions. Use complete sentences. Don't use contractions.

Efrain is sad. He is at his apartment but his apartment is empty (*vacio*). His brother is at work. His mother and father are also at work. His sisters are at school. His grandmother is in her bedroom. She is sleeping (*durmiendo*) because she is sick. His grandfather is at the park. Efrain has two dogs. His dogs are with (*con*) his grandfather. Efrain is lonely (*solitario*). He calls his friend. He feels better (*mejor*).

1. Where is Efrain?   He is at his apartment.
2. Where is his brother?   _____
3. Where are his parents?   _____
4. Where are his sisters?   _____
5. Where is his grandmother?   _____
6. Where is his grandfather?   _____
7. Where are his dogs?   _____

P1.j Directions: Look at Dulce's busy schedule. Then answer the questions. Use complete sentences. Don't use contractions. Check the table on page 12 to see when you need to use the and when you need to omit the.

6:00 a.m.	home
7:00 a.m.	Silver Gym
8:00 a.m.	work
9:00 a.m.	work
10:00 a.m.	work
11:00 a.m.	work
12:00 p.m.	Hoppers Restaurant
1:00 p.m.	school
2:00 p.m.	school
3:00 p.m.	school
4:00 p.m.	library
5:00 p.m.	supermarket
6:00 p.m.	home

1. Where is Dulce at 6:00 a.m.?   She is at home.
2. Where is Dulce at 7:00 a.m.?   _____
3. Where is Dulce at 8:00 a.m.?   _____
4. Where is Dulce at 12:00 p.m.?   _____
5. Where is Dulce at 1:00 p.m.?   _____
6. Where is Dulce at 4:00 p.m.?   _____
7. Where is Dulce at 5:00 p.m.?   _____
8. Where is Dulce at 6:00 p.m.?   _____

Chapter 2

What is Jose's date of birth?

When you apply for a job or go to the clinic for a doctor's appointment, you often need to answer questions such as your date of birth or the days you are available for your next appointment. This chapter teaches you how to answer these kinds of questions.

At the end of the chapter you will know how to
- ask and answer questions about when and what time activities take place.
- provide personal information such as your address, phone number, date of birth and country of origin.

Telling time in English is an extremely useful skill. Read this conversation.

Note the following:

▶ In response to the first question, you use the preposition **at** because you're telling what time an event takes place. You don't use the preposition **at** in response to the second question because you're simply stating the current time.

▶ The answers to each of the questions above begin with **it**. It is not correct to say ~~Is 8:30.~~ or ~~Is at 8:30.~~

When you respond to a **what time** question, you can repeat the subject or you can replace the subject with the pronoun **it**. For example, in response to the first question above, you can also say

▶ The party is at 8:30. (La fiesta es a las ocho y media.)

Questions made with **what time** and the verb **to be** have this form:

Question word	Verb to be	Rest of the sentence	Spanish translation
What time	**is**	**your appointment?**	¿A qué hora es tu cita?

You often include the time when you are talking about specific events. Study these words.

Vocabulary: Activities and events		
appointment (cita)	**class** (clase)	**meeting** (reunión)
work (trabajo)	**party** (fiesta)	**break** (descanso)

When you are talking about events, you often must specify what time the event starts and ends. To do this, you use **from** (de) and **to** (a). For example,

▶ My appointment is **from** 9:00 **to** 12:00. My appointment is **from** 9:00 – 12:00. (Mi cita es de las nueve a las doce.) (Mi cita es de nueve a doce.)

2.1.a Directions: Translate each word into Spanish.

1. work _trabajo_

2. appointment _____

3. break _____

4. party _____

5. meeting _____

6. class _____

2.1.b Directions: Translate each word into English.

1. cita _appointment_

2. clase _____

3. fiesta _____

4. reunión _____

5. trabajo _____

6. descanso _____

2.1.c Directions: Look at Amanda's schedule. Then answer the questions with a complete sentence. Make sure you include the preposition **at** in your answer.

9:00 a.m.	English class	3:00 p.m.	
10:00 a.m.		4:00 p.m.	meeting
11:00 a.m.	math class	5:00 p.m.	appointment with Luis Mendoza
12:00 a.m.		6:00 p.m.	
1:00 p.m.		7:00 p.m.	
2:00 p.m.	appointment with Dr. Dodd	8:00 p.m.	party

1. What time is the appointment with Dr. Dodd? _It is at 2:00 p.m._

2. What time is the party? _____

3. What time is the appointment with Luis Mendoza? _____

4. What time is the English class? _____

5. What time is the meeting? _____

6. What time is the math class? _____

2.1.d Directions: Translate these senences.

1. La reunión es a las seis.   The meeting is at 6:00.

2. Mi clase es a las ocho y media. _____

3. Tu cita es a las dos y cuarto. _____

4. La fiesta es de las nueve a las doce.   The party is at nine - twelve.

5. Nuestra cita es de las tres a las cuatro.   Our appt is et three - 4 oclock.

In this section you'll learn how to correctly specify days, months, and dates. Let's begin with some vocabulary. Remember that the pronunciation for each of these words is included in the dictionary in the back of this book.

Vocabulary: Days of the week with their abbreviations

Monday, Mon. (lunes)	**Tuesday, Tues.** (martes)	**Wednesday, Wed.** (miércoles)	**Thursday, Thurs.** (jueves)
Friday, Fri. (viernes)	**Saturday, Sat.** (sábado)	**Sunday, Sun.** (domingo)	

Vocabulary: Months of the year with their abbreviations

January, Jan. (enero)	**February, Feb.** (febrero)	**March, Mar.** (marzo)	**April, Apr.** (abril)
May (mayo)	**June** (junio)	**July,** (julio)	**August, Aug.** (agosto)
September, Sept. (septiembre)	**October, Oct.** (octubre)	**November, Nov.** (noviembre)	**December, Dec.** (diciembre)

Note the following:

► In English, unlike in Spanish, days of the week and months of the year are always capitalized.

► An abbreviation is always followed by a period (**.**).

Finally, study these times of the day.

Vocabulary: Time of the day

morning (mañana)	**afternoon** (tarde)	**evening***	**night** (noche)

*There is no Spanish translation for **evening**. In general it means the time between 5:00 p.m. and 8:00 p.m.

Writing Dates

There are many ways to write the date in English. Study these examples. Each one is correct.

August 2, 2010	**Aug. 2, 2010**	**8-2-2010**	**8/2/2010**

► In English, the month comes <u>before</u> the date. Thus, **8/2/2010** means **August 2, 2010**. It does not mean ~~February 8, 2010~~.

► You must place a comma <u>between</u> the day and the year. Thus, this date is not correct: ~~August 2 2010.~~

► You must place a period (**.**) after an abbreviation. Thus, this date is not correct: ~~Aug 2, 2010.~~

► You can either use slashes (**/**) or dashes (**-**) to separate the day, the month and the year. You cannot use slashes <u>and</u> dashes in the same date. These dates are not correct:

~~8/2-10.~~   ~~8-2/2010~~

2.2.a Directions: Write each date by spelling the name of the month. Do not use abbreviations.

1. 6/7/09   June 7, 2008
2. 1/3/10 _____
3. 11/12/99 _____

4. 8/17/06 _____
5. 7/21/12 _____
6. 9/1/96 _____

2.2.b Directions: Write each date by spelling the name of the month. Use abbreviations.

1. 8/24/08   Aug. 24, 2009
2. 3/3/13 _____
3. 10/10/07 _____

4. 12/1/99 _____
5. 2/2/12 _____
6. 4/19/86 _____

2.2.c Directions: Write each date using the mm/dd/yyyy format.

1. August 17, 1985   8/17/1985
2. May 7, 2012 _____
3. September 11, 2001 _____

4. July 16, 1969 _____
5. Nov. 25, 2006 _____
6. Dec. 25, 2012 _____

2.2.d Directions: Answer each question. You don't need to write a complete sentence.

1. What month is after (*después de*) February?   March
2. What day is before (*antes de*) Tuesday? _____
3. What day is before Saturday? _____
4. What day is after Wednesday? _____
5. What month is after July? _____
6. What month is before April? _____
7. What day is after Saturday? _____
8. What day is after Tuesday? _____
9. What month is before January? _____

2.2.e Directions: One of the dates in each line is not correct. Cross out the incorrect date.

1a. ~~3/3-2007~~
2a. April 4 2009
3a. 1-15-2010
4a. Feb 14 2009
5a. February 3 1999
6a. 7/17/09
7a. August 18, 2011
8a. 9/10/2009

1b. 3/3/2007
2b. April 4, 2009
3b. 1-15/2010
4b. Feb. 14, 2009
5b. February 3, 1999
6b. 7/17-09
7b. Aug 18, 2011
8b. 9/10 2009

Read this conversation.

Notice that this short conversation includes three different prepositions:

▶ You use the preposition **on** before the date, **July 23**, and before the day of the week, **Tuesday**.

▶ You use the preposition **at** before the time.

▶ You use the preposition **in** before the time of day, which, in this case, is **afternoon**. (Note that you use the preposition **at** before **night**.)

The prepositions used in the conversation are called ***prepositions of time***. Study this table to find out how to know which preposition of time to use.

Prepositions of time	Example	Spanish translation
Use **on** before days of the week	**on Monday**	el lunes
Use **on** before dates	**on February 22**	el 22 de febrero
Use **in** before months and years	**in March** **in 2010**	en Marzo en 2010
Use **in** before most times of the day	**in the morning** **in the afternoon** **in the evening**	de la mañana, por la manaña, de la tarde, por la tarde
Use **at** before *night*	**at night**	de la noche, por la noche
Use **at** before the time	**at 6:00**	a las seis

Questions made with **when** (cuándo) and the verb **to be** have this form:

Question word	Verb **to be**	Rest of the sentence	Spanish translation
When	**is**	**your appointment?**	¿Cuándo es tu cita?

When you respond to a *when question*, you can either repeat the subject or you can replace the subject with a subject pronoun. For example, in response to the question above, you can say

▶ My appointment is on June 25th.

▶ It is on June 25th.

Both responses are correct but the second response is more common. It is not correct to say,

▶ ~~Is on~~ June 25th.

2.3.a Directions: Complete each phrase with **on**, **in** or **at**.

1. __at__ 2:00
2. _____ Monday
3. _____ the morning
4. _____ 2010
5. _____ January 22, 2011
6. _____ Friday
7. _____ the afternoon
8. _____ 3:30
9. _____ the evening
10. _____ Saturday
11. _____ September 20
12. _____ 1998
13. _____ night
14. _____ June 16, 2009

2.3.b Directions: Read the appointment cards. Then answer each question with a complete sentence.

Dr. Mark Jones	Dr. Andrea Martin	Maria London
dentist	pediatrician	attorney (abogada)
Date: January 22	Date: August 30	Date: March 2
Time: 1:15 p.m.	Time: 4:30 p.m.	Time: 9 a.m.

1. When is the appointment with Dr. Jones? — It is on January 22.
2. What time is the appointment with Dr. Jones? _____
3. When is the appointment with Dr. Martin? _____
4. What time is the appointment with Dr. Martin? _____
5. What time is the appointment with Ms. London? _____
6. When is the appointment with Ms. London? _____

2.3.c Directions: Complete each sentence with **on**, **in** or **at**.

1. The party is __on__ Tuesday __at__ 3:00.
2. The meeting is _____ 8:00 _____ night.
3. I am tired _____ the morning.
4. My trip (*viaje*) is _____ September.
5. The party isn't _____ night. It's _____ the morning.
6. Her appointment is _____ March 2.
7. She is hungry _____ the evening.
8. The meeting is _____ 4:00 _____ Wednesday.

2.3.d Directions: Complete each sentence with **from**, **to** or **at**.

1. My meeting is from 2:00 __to__ 3:00.
2. My math class is _____ 6:30.
3. Our break is _____ 9:00.
4. Her break is from 10:00 _____ 10:30.
5. Their appointment is _____ 7:30 to 8:00.
6. I work _____ 8:00 _____ 5:00.

2.4 *What* Questions

Many questions that are used to ask for information begin with **what** (qué or cuál). Questions made with **what** (qué or cuál) and the verb **to be** have this form:

Interrogativo	Verbo to be	Resto de la oración	Traducción en español
What	is	your name?	¿Cuál es tu nombre? ¿Cómo te llamas?

You can use a contraction to shorten **what is** to **what's**. Both of these questions have the same meaning:

▶ What's your name?

▶ What is your name?

The following list includes words that you may need to know when completing forms or answering personal questions. You'll use these words in the exercises on the next page.

Vocabulary: Personal information

first name (nombre)	**last name** (apellido)	**middle name** (segundo nombre)
complete name/full name (nombre completo)	**middle initial** (la inicial del segundo nombre)	**street address** (dirección)
city (ciudad)	**state** (estado)	**country** (país)
zip code (código postal)	**area code** (código de área)	**telephone number** (número de teléfono)
date of birth (fecha de nacimiento)	**birthday** (cumpleaños)	**place of birth** (lugar de nacimiento)
job/occupation (trabajo)	**Social Security Number** (número de Seguro Social)	**age** (edad)

Note:

▶ The *area code* is the 3 digits that precede a phone number.

▶ The *zip code* is the postal code that is placed after the state. The zip code is usually six digits but sometimes is ten digits.

▶ *Date of birth* and *birthday* are not the same thing. For example, if your date of birth is **June 22, 1980,** your birthday would be **June 22.**

2.4.a Directions: Underline the item that best fits the description.

1. **Zip code**   a. <u>46578</u>   b. 423   c. 656-456-3421
2. **Date of birth** a. 5/6/91   b. May 6   c. May, 1991
3. **Middle initial** a. Macias   b. M.   c. Daniel
4. **Birthplace**   a. Puebla, Mexico   b. 7/22/86   c. 22 River Road
5. **Job**   a. Hawaii   b. United States   c. engineer
6. **Area code**   a. 46578   b. 816   c. 816-678-8865

2.4.b Directions: Write the letter that describes the information in column 1.

1. M. _f_   a. Last name
2. nurse _____   b. Date of birth
3. 55897 _____   c. City
4. 212 _____   d. Street address
5. 457 64 5356 _____   e. Birthday
6. Lopez _____   f. Middle initial
7. Los Angeles _____   g. State
8. July 22 _____   h. Job
9. California _____   i. Country
10. United States _____   j. Zip code
11. 444 Main Street _____   k. Area code
12. Artemio _____   l. Social Security Number
13. 7/5/1990 _____   m. First name
14. Artemio M. López _____   n. Complete name

2.4.c Directions: Look at the identification card. Then, answer the questions. Use complete sentences.

Last name _Montes_ **First name** _Francisco_ **Middle initial** _N._
Street address _2342 6th Ave._ **City** _Redwood City_ **State** _CA_
Zip code _95014_ **Telephone number** _650-555-1234_
Job _construction worker_ **Date of birth** _8/3/87_
Birthplace _Moralia, México_

1. What is Francisco's last name?   His last name is Montes.

2. What is Francisco's street address?   _____

3. What is Francisco's job?   _____

4. What is Francisco's date of birth?   _____

5. What is Francisco's birthplace?   _____

6. What is Francisco's area code?   _____

7. What is Francisco's zip code?   _____

8. When is Francisco's birthday?   _____

2.5 Possessive Nouns

Suppose you need to give personal information about someone other than yourself. To do that, you use *possessive nouns.* Read this conversation. Note the following:

What is Jose's date of birth?
(¿Cuál es la fecha de nacimiento de José?)

His date of birth is September 15, 2009.
(Su fecha de nacimiento es el 15 de septiembre, 2009.)

► In this conversation, the possessive noun is **Jose's**. You use possessive nouns to talk about something that belongs to or pertains to someone else.

► You also could have answered the question:

Jose's date of birth is September 15, 2009

Grammar recipe: How to make a possessive noun:

► If the possessor is singular place an **'s** after the possessor's name, followed by what is possessed (For example, **Susan's car**.).

Here are some examples:

English	Spanish
Laura's telephone number is 643-434-0342.	El número de teléfono de Laura es 643-434-0342.
My daughter's birthday is May 2.	El cumpleaños de mi hija es el 2 de mayo.
Juan's sofa is new.	El sofá de Juan es nuevo.
Lisa's job is difficult.	El trabajo de Lisa es difícil.
The teacher's car is broken.	El carro de la maestra está roto.

2.5.a Directions: One of the phrases in each line is not correct. Cross out the incorrect phrase.

1a. ~~The book of Lucy~~	1b. Lucy's book
2a. Anna's house	2b. The house of Anna
3a. Lisa's car	3b. The car of Lisa
4a. Chris' backpack	4b. The backpack of Chris
5a. The doctor of Mrs. Wilson	5b. Mrs. Wilson's doctor
6a. The dog of Martin	6b. Martin's dog
7a. Edgar's girlfriend	7b. Edgar girlfriend
8a. The teacher of Antonio	8b. Antonio's teacher

2.5.b Directions: Rewrite each sentence so it is correct.

1. The book of Antonio is interesting.   Antonio's book is interesting.

2. The car of Rodolfo is broken.

3. The house of Jackie is on Union Street.

4. The shoes of Alba are from Mexico.

5. The bedroom of Sandra is very clean.

6. The cousin of Juana is handsome.

7. The father of Pedro is sick.

8. The class of Barbara is interesting.

2.5.c Directions: Read the story. Then write **T** if the statement is *true* and **F** if the statement is *false*.

Ana has one sister and one brother. Ana's sister is 23 years old. Her name is Emily. Emily is an artist. Emily's husband is Mario. Mario is an engineer. Ana's brother is 18 years old. His name is Porferio. Porferio isn't married. But he has a dog. Porferio's dog is very big and very noisy (*ruidoso*). He also has a cat. Porferio's cat is very quiet (*silencioso*).

1. Ana's sister is Annette. _F_

2. Ana's sister is 18 years old. _____

3. Ana's brother is Porferio. _____

4. Porferio is married. _____

5. Porferio's dog is big. _____

6. Porferio's cat is noisy. _____

2.5.d Directions: Translate these sentences.

1. La casa de Ana es bonita.   Ana's house is beautiful.

2. El carro de Ernesto es azul.

3. El vestido de Emily es caro.

4. La niña de Mónica tiene ocho años.

5. La prima de Eva es enfermera.

6. El padre de Nick está en el trabajo.

2.6 *Question Word* Questions **vs.** *Yes/No* Questions

In this book, we discuss two kinds of questions: *Yes/no* questions and *question word* questions. Read this conversation:

Notice the following:

▶ The first question is a *yes/no question*, and the response is either **yes** or **no**.

▶ The second question is a *question word question*, that is, it starts with a question word, which, in this case, is **where**.

Grammar Recipe: How to distinguish *yes/no questions* from *question word questions*:

▶ *Yes/no questions* usually start with a form of the verb **to be (is** or **are)**, followed by a noun or pronoun.

▶ *Question word questions* usually start with a question word, such as **where** (dónde), **when** (cuándo), **what** (qué or cuál) or **what time** (qué hora or a qué hora).

To help you understand the differences between these kinds of questions and how to answer them, study these charts.

Yes/no questions	Answers
Are you tired? (¿Estás cansado?) (¿Estás cansada?)	**Yes, I am.** (Sí.) **No, I'm not. No, I am not.** (No.)
Is your sister a nurse? (¿Tu hermana es enfermera?)	**Yes, she is.** (Sí.) **No, she isn't. No, she is not.** (No.)
Are your parents at work? (¿Tus padres están en el trabajo?)	**Yes, they are.** (Sí.) **No, they aren't. No, they are not.** (No.)

Question word questions	Answers
What is your name? (¿Cuál es tu nombre?)	**My name is Raoul Parks.** (Mi nombre es Raoul Parks.)
When is your birthday (¿Cuándo es tu cumpleaños?)	**My birthday is May 2.** (Mi cumpleaños es el segundo de mayo.)
How old are you? (¿Cuántos años tienes?)	**I am 24 years old.** (Tengo 24 años.)
Where is your book? (¿Dónde está tu libro?)	**It is on the table.** (Está en la mesa.)

2.6.a Directions: Underline the correct answer.

1. **What time is the movie?**   1a. <u>It is at 6:30.</u>   1b. It is in Redwood City.

2. **Is your teacher at school?**   2a. She is a teacher.   2b. No, she isn't.

3. **When is your class?**   3a. It is on Mondays.   3b. It is at Hoover School.

4. **Is Juana a nurse?**   4a. No, she isn't.   4b. She is at work.

5. **Where is your appointment?**   5a. It is on Thursday.   5b. It is at our school.

6. **When is your soccer game?**   6a. It is on Mondays.   6b. It is at Blaine School.

7. **Where is the supermarket?**   7a. It is on Beacon Street.   7b. Yes, it is.

8. **What time is your meeting?**   8a. It is at 2:00.   8b. Yes, it is.

2.6.b Directions: Read the conversation between a husband, Julio, and his wife, Ana, talking on their cell phones. Then answer the questions. Use complete sentences. Use contractions when you can.

Julio: Where are you?

Ana: I am at home.

Julio: Where is Peter?

Ana: He is at work.

Julio: What time is Peter's appointment?

Ana: It is at 8:00.

Julio: Where is Soledad?

Ana: She is at Myra's house.

Julio: Where is Sebastian?

Ana: He is at the park.

Julio: Are you alone (*sola*)?

Ana: No, I'm not. I have company (*compañía*).

Julio: Who? (*¿Quién?*)

Ana: My friend, Louisa.

1. Where is Ana?   She is at home.

2. Is Peter at home? _____

3. What time is Peter's appointment? _____

4. Is Soledad at Myra's house? _____

5. Where is Sebastian? _____

6. Is Ana alone? _____

7. Is Louisa Ana's mother? _____

8. Is Julio at home? _____

📖 Chapter 2 Summary

Prepositions of time

You use *prepositions of time* to tell when an event takes place.

Prepositions of time	Example	Spanish translation
Use **on** before days of the week	**on Monday**	el lunes
Use **on** before dates	**on February 22**	el 22 de febrero
Use **in** before months and years	**in March** **in 2010**	en Marzo, en 2010
Use **in** before most times of the day	**in the morning** **in the afternoon** **in the evening**	de la mañana, por la manaña de la tarde, por la tarde
Use **at** before *night*	**at night**	de la noche, por la noche
Use **at before** the time	**at 6:00**	a las seis

Dates

All of the following are correct ways to write dates in English.

August 2, 2010	**Aug. 2, 2010**	**8-2-2010**	**8/2/2010**

Question word questions

Question word questions with the verb **to be** have this form:

Question word	Verb to be	Rest of the sentence	Spanish translation
What time	**is**	**your appointment?**	¿A qué hora es tu cita?*
When	**is**	**your appointment?**	¿Cuándo es tu cita?
What	**is**	**your name?**	¿Cuál es tu nombre? ¿Cómo te llamas?

Possessive nouns

You use *possessive nouns* to talk about something that belongs to or pertains to someone else. To make a possessive noun:

▶ If the possessor is singular and does not end in **s,** place an **'s** after the possessor's name, followed by what is possessed (For example, **Susan's car**).

 **More Practice!**

P2.a Directions: Answer each question. You don't need to write a complete sentence.

1. What month is after July? _____ August _____
2. What month is before July? _____
3. What day is before Sunday? _____
4. What day is after Sunday? _____
5. What year is before 2011? _____
6. What month is before December? _____
7. What month is before May? _____
8. What day is after Thursday? _____
9. What day is between Thursday and Saturday? _____
10. What year is after 2013? _____

P2.b Directions: Complete each sentence with **on**, **in** or **at**.

1. The meeting is __on__ Thursday __at__ 8:00 a.m.
2. Your shoes are _____ the bedroom.
3. The class is _____ 8:00 _____ Brower Adult School.
4. The party is _____ Tortilla Flat restaurant.
5. I am tired _____ the afternoon.
6. My meeting is _____ San Francisco.
7. My keys are _____ home _____ the kitchen.
8. My appointment is _____ Thursday.
9. I am _____ work.
10. My appointment with Dr. Jackson is _____ 6:30 _____ Friday.
11. My birthday is _____ September.
12. My class is _____ Wednesday _____ the afternoon.

P2.c Directions: Complete each sentence with **from**, **to** or **at**.

1. My meeting is __from__ 8:45 __to__ 10:00.
2. Her break is from 10:00 _____ 10:30.
3. My math class is _____ 6:30.
4. Their appointment is _____ 7:30 _____ 8:00.
5. Your break is _____ 11:30 _____ 12:00.
6. Lilia's party is _____ 9:00.

P2.d Directions: Arrange the words so that they make a question. Don't forget to end each question with a question mark(**?**).

1. apartment / your / is / Where <u>Where</u> <u>is</u> <u>your</u> <u>apartment?</u>

2. When / your / is / meeting _____ _____ _____ _____

3. party / What time / the / is _____ _____ _____ _____

4. sister / Where / your / is _____ _____ _____ _____

5. When / class / Juan's / is _____ _____ _____ _____

6. house / is / Where / Jose's _____ _____ _____ _____

7. is / your / What / job _____ _____ _____ _____

8. What / date of birth / is / her _____ _____ _____ _____

P2.e Directions: Look at the identification card. Then, answer the questions. Use complete sentences.

Last name _Ramirez_ **First name** _Gabriela_ **Middle initial** _S._
Street address _11 West Ave._ **City** _Brooklyn_ **State** _NY_
Zip code _10011_ **Telephone number** _212-555-4564_
job _secretary_ **Date of birth** _2/1/82_
birthplace _San Salvador, El Salvador_

1. What is Gabriela's last name?   Her last name is Ramirez.

2. What is Gabriela's area code?   _____

3. Is Gabriela a teacher?   _____

4. What is Gabriela's date of birth?   _____

5. What is Gabriela's birthplace?   _____

6. Is Gabriela's birthday January 2?   _____

P2.f Directions: Rewrite each sentence so it is correct.

1. The house of Lana is new.   Lana's house is new.

2. The cell phone of Ken is broken.   _____

3. The microwave of Adam is old.   _____

4. The brother of Claudia is handsome.   _____

5. The bedroom of Betty is very big.   _____

6. The car of Laura is expensive.   _____

7. The teacher of Maribel is interesting.   _____

8. The son of Eva is sick.   _____

9. The cousin of Chris is divorced.   _____

10. The dress of Ariana is beautiful.   _____

P2.g Directions: Read the story. Then answer the questions. Use complete sentences. Use contractions when you can.

It is Tuesday. Jana Aguilar is not at work. She is at home. She is sick. She also is very tired. She has an appointment at 9:00 at the clinic. Jana's doctor is Dr. Johnson. Dr. Johnson examines Jana. He says (*dice*), "Jana, you have the flu." (*la gripe*).

1. What day is it?   It's Tuesday.

2. What is Jana's last name?

3. Is Jana at work?

4. What time is Jana's appointment?

5. Where is Jana's appointment?

6. Is Jana sick?

P2.h Directions: One of the items in each line is not correct. Cross out the incorrect item.

1a. ~~3/1 2007~~	1b. 3/1/2007
2a. June 22, 2009	2b. June 22 2009
3a. 2-15/2010	3b. 2-15-2010
4a. Dec 26, 2012	4b. Dec. 26, 2012
5a. February 3 1989	5b. February 3, 1989
6a. at morning	6b. in the morning
7a. in the afternoon	7b. at the afternoon
8a. at night	8b. at the night
9a. at 7:30	9b. in 7:30
10a. at the Chavez Restaurant	10b. at Chavez Restaurant
11a. at home	11b. at the home
12a. at the Ling Pharmacy (*farmacia*)	12b. at Ling Pharmacy
13a. on Monday	13b. the Monday
14a. from 9:00 to 5:00	14b. from 9:00 a 5:00

P2.i Directions: Translate these sentences.

1. La hermana de Pablo es bonita.   Pablo's sister is beautiful.

2. El carro de Ángel es azul.

3. La clase es a las nueve.

4. Las llaves están en la cocina.

5. Estoy en Los Ángeles.

6. Estamos en la casa de Bruno.

7. Mi cita es el lunes.

8. Mi cumpleaños es en julio.

9. Tu descanso es de las diez a las diez
    y media.

10. Tu mochila está en la oficina.

Chapter 3

There's a pizza in the oven.

Conversation often requires you to give people information. For example, you may need to tell your boss that there is a problem in the kitchen. Or you may need to tell the students in your English class that there are more books in the cabinet. To do this, you often use the expressions **there is** (hay) and **there are** (hay).

At the end of this chapter you will know how to

- use **there is** and **there are** to describe the current state of things.
- ask and answer questions that include **there is** and **there are.**

In everyday conversation, it is very common to use the expressions **there is** (hay) and **there are** (hay) to describe the current state of things. Read this conversation:

Notice that, in Spanish, you use hay to refer to a singular noun or a plural noun. In English you use **there is** to refer to a singular noun and **there are** to refer to a plural noun. Becuse there is only one pizza, you say

▶ **There is** a pizza in the oven. (Hay una pizza en el horno.)

But you say

▶ **There are** drinks in the refrigerador. (Hay bebidas en el refrigerador.)

because there is more than one drink.

Cuidado: **There** has two different meanings. It means hay. It also means ahí, allí, and allá, You can say, for example, **The book is there.** (El libro está allá.)

Sentences with **there is** and t**here are** have this form:

There	is or are	Rest of the sentence	Spanish translation
There	is	a pizza in the oven.	Hay una pizza en el horno.
There	are	pizzas in the oven.	Hay pizzas en el horno.

When referring to a singular noun, you must include **a** or **an**. For example,

▶ There is **a** chair in the office. (Hay una silla en la oficina.)

It is not correct to say,

▶ ~~There is chair in the office.~~

When referring to more than one object, you do not use **a** or **an**. These sentences are correct:

▶ There are chairs in the office. (Hay sillas en la oficina.)
▶ There are three chairs in the office. (Hay tres sillas en la oficina.)

These sentences are not correct:

▶ ~~There are chair in the office.~~
▶ ~~There are a chair in the office.~~

3.1.a Directions: Complete each sentence using **There is** or **There are**.

1. _____There is_____ a backpack on the table.

2. _____ a cook in the kitchen.

3. _____ six chairs in their living room.

4. _____ children in the classroom (*aula*).

5. _____ a school next to my house.

6. _____ a television in front of the couch.

3.1.b Directions: One of the sentences in each pair is not a correct sentence. Cross out the incorrect sentence.

1a. There is a fly (*mosca*) in your soup.   1b. ~~There are a fly in your soup.~~
2a. There are students from Mexico in my class.   2b. There is students from Peru in my class.
3a. There is a toy on the chair.   3b. There are a toy on the chair.
4a. There are a dogs in the garden.   4b. There are dogs in the garden.
5a. There are a six children at the park.   5b. There are six children at the park.
6a. There are a TV in the kitchen.   6b. There is a TV in the kitchen.
7a. There are two sofas in the living room.   7b. There is two sofas in the living room.
8a. There is an end table next to the couch.   8b. There is end table next to the couch.

3.1.c Directions: Change the subject of the sentence from singular to plural. Don't forget to change the verb also.

1. There is a dog in the living room.   _There are dogs in the living room._

2. There is a cat in the kitchen.   _____

3. There is an eraser in my backpack.   _____

4. There is a table in my bedroom.   _____

5. There is a chair in front of the sofa.   _____

6. There is a sock on the floor.   _____

7. There is a pizza in the oven.   _____

8. There is a backpack next to the TV.   _____

3.1.d Directions: Translate these sentences.

1. Hay un perro en el baño.   _There is a dog in the bathroon._

2. Hay dos baños en la casa.   _____

3. Hay zapatos debajo de la cama.   _____

4. Hay tres lápices en la mesa.   _____

5. Hay una mochila al lado de la puerta.   _____

In English, contractions are often used to shorten what you want to say. The contraction for **there** and **is** is **there's**. Note that **there is** and **there's** mean the same thing. Study these examples:

Sentences without contractions	Sentences with contractions	Spanish translation
There is a pizza on the table.	**There's a pizza on the table.**	Hay una pizza en la mesa.
There is a car next to your house.	**There's a car next to your house.**	Hay un carro al lado de tu casa.

There is no contraction that joins **there** and **are**. Thus this sentence isn't correct:

▸ ~~There're two chairs in my kitchen.~~

There vs. They

Many people confuse **they** and **there**. Even though these words sound similar they are pronounced differently. (**They** is pronounced déi and **there is** pronounced der.) Remember that **they** means ellos or ellas and **there** followed by **is** or **are** means hay. This sentence is correct:

▸ There are cookies in the kitchen. (Hay galletas en la cocina.)

This sentence has no meaning.

▸ ~~They are cookies in the kitchen.~~

Here are more examples:

Correct sentences	Incorrect sentences
There are dogs in the park. (Hay perros en el parque.)	~~They are dogs in the park.~~
They are from Chile. (Ellos son de Chile.)	~~There are from Chile.~~

There vs. They're

In English it is common for two words to have the same pronunciations but different meanings and spellings. These words are called *homonyms*. **There** and **they're** are *homonyms*. That is, they have the same pronunciation but different meanings. Study this table.

English	Spanish	Example
there	hay	**There is a TV in our living room.** (Hay un televisor en nuestra sala.)
they're	ellos son, ellos están, ellas son, ellas están	**They're married.** (Ellos están casados.)

3.2.a Directions: Rewrite each sentence, using a contraction. If there is no contraction, write **No contraction.**

1. There is a towel in the bathroom.   There's a towel in the bathroom.

2. There are 26 students in my class.   No contraction.

3. There is an orange in the kitchen.

4. There is a cat in that classroom.

5. There are backpacks next to the window.

6. There are two eggs on the counter.

7. There is a restaurant next to my school.

8. There is a ball on the floor.

3.2.b Directions: Complete each sentence using **There** or **They**.

1. They   are from Nicaragua.

2. _____   are lamps in my bedroom.

3. _____   are two pencils in my backpack.

4. _____   are not at school.

5. _____   are 22 years old.

6. _____   are many (*muchas*) people in the park today (*hoy*).

3.2.c Directions: Complete each sentence using **There are** or **They're**.

1. They're   from Oregon.

2. _____   peaches on the table.

3. _____   shoes on the bed.

4. _____   my friends.

5. _____   at work now.

6. _____   many people at the meeting.

3.2.d Directions: One of the sentences in each pair is not a correct sentence. Cross out the incorrect sentence.

1a. There are dogs in the kitchen.   1b. ~~There're dogs in the kitchen.~~
2a. There're students from China in my class. 2b. There are students from China in my class.
3a. There are notebooks on the table.   3b. There're notebooks on the table.
4a. There's a microwave in the kitchen.   4b. Theres a microwave in the kitchen.
5a. They is a dresser in the living room.   5b. There is a dresser in the living room.
6a. They are two beds in the bedroom.   6b. There are two beds in the bedroom.
7a. There is a dog under the table.   7b. They are a dog under the table.

Negative Statements: *There isn't* and *There aren't*

Now that you know about affirmative sentences with **there is** and **there are**, you're ready to create negative sentences. To make a negative sentence from a sentence that includes **there is**

▶ Change **there is** to **there is not** or **there isn't**.

To make a negative sentence from a sentence that includes **there are**

▶ Change **there are** to **there are not** or **there aren't**.

Here are some examples of affirmative and negative statements.

	Affirmative statements	Negative statements
Singular	There is a pencil on the table.	There is not a pencil on the table.
	There's a pencil on the table.	There isn't a pencil on the table.
	(Hay un lápiz en la mesa.)	(No hay un lápiz en la mesa.)
Plural	There are pencils on the table.	There are not pencils on the table.
	(Hay lápices en la mesa.)	There aren't pencils on the table.
		(No hay lápices en la mesa.)

Study this vocabulary. You'll use these words in the exercises on the next page.

dress (vestido) **shoes** (zapatos) **jacket** (chaqueta)

shirt (camisa) **blouse** (blusa) **hat** (sombrero)

pants* (pantalones) **socks** (calcetines) **coat** (abrigo)

*__Pants__ (pantalones) is always plural. Thus, even when you only have one pair of pants you say

▶ **My pants are new.** (Mis pantalones son nuevos.)

3.3.a Directions: Change each sentence from affirmative to negative. Use contractions when you can.

1. There is a hat on the sofa.   There isn't a hat on the sofa.
2. There is a sock on the floor.
3. There is a jacket in the living room.
4. There is a coat next to the chair.
5. There are eggs in the kitchen.
6. There are shoes on the floor.
7. There are lamps in our bedroom.
8. There are pants in the dresser.

3.3.b Directions: Look at the picture. Then write six affirmative sentences about what is on the bed. Use contractio

1.   There's a hat on the bed.
2.
3.
4.
5.
6.

3.3.c Directions: Translate these sentences. Use contractions when you can.

1. No hay un abrigo en el piso.   There isn't a coat on the floor.
2. No hay chaquetas en el sofá.
3. No hay un hombre delante de la escuela.
4. No hay borradores en mi mochila.
5. No hay estudiantes en la playa.

You know how to use **there is** and **there are** in affirmative and negative statements. Now you're ready to use **there is** and **there are** to ask questions.

Grammar recipe:

▶ To ask a question to determine if one thing exists, start the question with **Is there**.

▶ To ask a question to determine if more than one thing exists, start the question with **Are there**.

The following chart illustrates the difference between statements and questions. Notice that statements start with **There is** or **There are** and questions start with **Is there** or **Are there**.

Statements	Questions
There is a sock on the floor. **There's a sock on the floor.** (Hay un calcetín en el piso.)	**Is there a sock on the floor?** (¿Hay un calcetín en el piso?)
There are socks on the floor. (Hay calcetines en el piso.)	**Are there socks on the floor?** (¿Hay calcetines en el piso?)

Note that, in the example above, you need to include **a** before **sock** because you are talking about one sock. When you talk about more than one sock, you don't include **a**.

Count and noncount nouns

Most nouns are *count nouns* because they can easily be counted. For example, it's easy to count one apple, two apples, and so on. A *noncount noun* is a noun that is not easily counted. **Noncount** nouns are singular but aren't preceded by **a** or **an**. **Rice** (arroz) is a noncount noun. So you say,

▶ There isn't rice. (No hay arroz.)

You don't say

▶ ~~There isn't a rice.~~ ~~(No hay un arroz.)~~

Here are several examples of foods that are noncount nouns.

bread (pan)	**rice** (arroz)	**fruit** (fruta)	**meat** (carne)
ice cream (helado)	**milk** (leche)	**juice** (jugo)	**cheese** (queso)

3.4.a Directions: In the first column write **Q** if the sentence is a *question* (*pregunta*) and **S** if the sentence is a *statement* (*declaración*). In the second column, put a period (.) or a question mark (?).

	Is this sentence a *question* or a *statement*?	Punctuation
1. Is there a book on the table	1a. _Q_	1b. _?_
2. There is a book on the table	2a. _____	2b. _____
3. Is there a microwave in your kitchen	3a. _____	3b. _____
4. There's a microwave in my kitchen	4a. _____	4b. _____
5. There are apples in the refrigerator	5a. _____	5b. _____
6. Are there apples in the refrigerator	6a. _____	6b. _____

3.4.b Directions: Change each statement to a question.
1. There is a dog in the living room.   Is there a dog in the living room?
2. There are dogs in the living room.
3. There is rice on the table.
4. There are maps in your classroom.
5. There is meat in the microwave.
6. There is cheese on the table.
7. There are students in the classroom.

3.4.c Directions: One of the sentences in each pair is not a correct sentence. Cross out the incorrect sentence.

1a. There is cheese on the table.   1b. ~~There is a cheese on the table.~~
2a. Is there a meat in the oven?   2b. Is there meat in the oven?
3a. There is a rice on the floor.   3b. There is rice on the floor.
4a. There are a students from China in my class.   4b. There are students from China in my class.
5a. Is there a doctor here?   5b. Is there a doctor here.
6a. There are a dogs at the park.   6b. There are dogs at the park.

3.4.d Directions: Write **count** or **noncount** next to each noun.
1. rice _____noncount_____
2. bread _____
3. book _____
4. pencil _____
5. cheese _____
6. microwave _____
7. milk_____
8. couch _____
9. dress _____
10. money _____

In the previous section you learned to ask questions that start with **Is there** and **Are there**. These questions are called *yes/no questions* because your answer often begins with **yes** or **no**. Study this conversation.

Notice that, in the above conversation, you also could give long answers. For example, the responses could be

▸ Yes, there is a pizza in the oven./ Yes there's a pizza in the oven.

▸ No, there are not drinks in the refrigerator./No there aren't drinks in the refrigerator.

This table summarizes how to answer **there is** and **there are** questions using short answers.

Answering *yes/no questions* using short answers	
Is there a sock on the floor? (¿Hay un calcetín en el piso?)	**Are there socks on the floor?** (¿Hay calcetines en el piso?)
Yes, there is. (Sí, hay.) **No, there is not.** (No, no hay.) **No, there isn't.** (No, no hay.)	**Yes, there are.** (Sí, hay.) **No, there are not.** (No, no hay.) **No, there aren't.** (No, no hay.)

Notice that you can use a contraction for a negative short answer. Thus you can say

▸ No, there isn't. (No, no hay.)

▸ No, there aren't. (No, no hay.)

You cannot use a contraction in an affirmative short answer.

▸ ~~Yes, there's.~~

▸ ~~Yes, there're.~~

3.5.a Directions: Look at the picture below. First respond to each question using a long answer. Use contractions when you can. Then, use one of the following short answers:

Yes, there is.   Yes, there are.

No, there isn't.   No, there aren't.

1. Is there cheese on the table?	1a. <u>Yes, there's cheese on the table.</u>
	1b. <u>Yes, there is.</u>
2. Is there a dog under the table?	2a. _____
	2b. _____
3. Are there shoes on the table?	3a. _____
	3b. _____
4. Is there a broom next to the table?	4a. _____
	4b. _____
5. Is there a ball in front of the dog?	5a. _____
	5b. _____

3.5.b Directions: Only one of the responses to each question is grammatically correct. Underline the correct response.

1. Is there a pen in your backpack?
    a. <u>Yes, there is.</u>   b. Yes, there are.

2. Are there pencils in your backpack?
    a. Yes, there is.   b. Yes, there are.

3. Are there students from Peru in your class?
    a. No, there isn't.   b. No, there aren't.

4. Is there a priest (*sacerdote*) at church?
    a. Yes, there is.   b. Yes, there are.

5. Are there doctors at the hospital?
    a. No, there are.   b. No, there aren't.

6. Is there a pizza in the oven?
    a. No, there aren't.   b. No, there isn't.

7. Are there many children at the party?
    a. Yes, there're.   b. Yes, there are.

8. Is there a shoe under the table?
    a. Yes, there's.   b. Yes, there is.

The answer to a *yes/no question* is either **yes** or **no**. But what you say after **yes** or **no** depends on the question. Look at these examples.

The key to answering *yes/no questions* correctly is to pay attention to the first few words of the question.

- ▶ In the first example above, the question starts with **Are there**, so you include **there are** in the answer.
- ▶ In the second example above, the question begins with a form of the verb **to be** followed by a noun or pronoun, so the answer includes a form of the verb **to be** preceded by a noun or pronoun.

Here are more examples.

Questions that start with **Is there** or **Are there**	Questions that start with the verb **to be** followed by a noun or pronoun*
Is there a school next to your house? (¿Hay una escuela al lado de tu casa?)	**Is** the school next to your house? (¿La escuela está al lado de tu casa?)
Yes, there is. (Sí.) **No, there isn't.** (No, no hay.) **No, there is not.** (No, no hay.)	**Yes, it is.** (Sí.) **No, it isn't.** (No.) **No, it is not.** (No.)
Is there a book on the table? (¿Hay un libro en la mesa?)	**Is** your book on the table? (¿Tu libro está en la mesa?)
Yes, there is. (Sí.) **No, there isn't.** (No, no hay.) **No, there is not.** (No, no hay.)	**Yes, it is.** (Sí.) **No, it isn't.** (No.) **No, it is not.** (No.)
Are there pizzas in the oven? (¿Hay pizzas en el horno?)	**Are** the pizzas in the oven? (¿Las pizzas están en el horno?)
Yes, there are. (Sí.) **No, there aren't.** (No, no hay.) **No, there are not.** (No, no hay.)	**Yes, they are.** (Sí.) **No, they aren't.** (No.) **No, they are not.** (No.)

*For more about answering *yes/no* questions that start with the verb **to be**, see *Gramática del inglés: Paso a paso 1*.

3.6.a Directions: Only one of the responses to each question is grammatically correct. Underline the correct response.

1. **Are your parents in the United States?**
   1a. <u>Yes, they are.</u>   1b. Yes, there are.   1c. Yes, they're.

2. **Are you married?**
   2a. Yes, I'm.   2b. Yes, there is.   2c. Yes, I am.

3. **Are your friends at the park?**
   3a. Yes, there aren't.   3b. No, they aren't.   3c. No, they not.

4. **Is there cheese in the refrigerator?**
   4a. No, there isn't.   4b. No, it isn't.   4c. No, there is no.

5. **Are there students from Africa in your class?**
   5a. Yes, they are.   5b. Yes, there are.   5c. Yes, there is.

6. **Is Bernardo a good husband?**
   6a. Yes, he is.   6b. Yes, they are.   6c. No, they aren't.

7. **Are there shoes under the dresser?**
   7a. Yes, they are.   7b. Yes, there is.   7c. Yes, there are.

8. **Are the students hardworking?**
   8a. No, there aren't.   8b. No, they aren't.   8c. No, they are.

3.6.b Directions: Read the paragraph below. Then answer the questions. Use complete sentences. Use contractions when you can.

Nina and Gaby are sisters. They are from El Salvador. Nina is a student. She is 21 years old. Gaby is a nurse. She is 24 years old. Nina and Gaby are single. They have an apartment. They are very happy in their apartment. There are three rooms in their apartment. The living room is big. There is a couch, two end tables, a TV, a lamp and two chairs. The bedroom is very small. There is only one bed and one small dresser. The kitchen is perfect. It has a microwave, a good stove and a big refrigerator.

1. Is Nina married?   No, she isn't.

2. Is Gaby single?

3. What is Gaby's job?

4. Is Nina a student?

5. Where are they from?

6. Are there three rooms in their apartment?

7. Is the living room small?

8. Are there four chairs in the living room?

9. Are there two beds in the bedroom?

10. Are they happy in their apartment?

Affirmative and negative sentences with **there is** and **there are** have this form:

	Singular	Plural
Affirmative statements	**There is a pencil on the table.** **There's a pencil on the table.** (Hay un lápiz en la mesa.)	**There are pencils on the table.** (Hay lápices en la mesa.)
Negative statements	**There is not a pencil on the table.** **There isn't a pencil on the table.** (No hay un lápiz en la mesa.)	**There are not pencils on the table. There aren't pencils on the table.** (No hay lápices en la mesa.)

Questions with **is there** and **are there**--and their answers--have this form:

Answering *yes/no* questions using short answers	
Is there a sock on the floor? (¿Hay un calcetín en el piso?) **Yes, there is.** (Sí, hay.) **No, there is not.** (No, no hay.) **No, there isn't.** (No, no hay.)	**Are there socks on the floor?** (¿Hay calcetines en el piso?) **Yes, there are.** (Sí, hay.) **No, there are not.** (No, no hay.) **No, there aren't.** (No, no hay.)

The following table shows how to responde to *yes/no* questions that start with the **Is there** and **Are there** and *yes/no* questions that start with the verb **to be**.

Questions that start with **Is there** or **Are there**	Questions that start with the verb **to be** followed by a noun or pronoun
Is there a school next to your house? (¿Hay una escuela al lado de tu casa?) **Yes, there is.** (Sí.) **No, there isn't.** (No, no hay.) **No, there is not.** (No, no hay.)	**Is the school next to your house?** (¿La escuela está al lado de tu casa?) **Yes, it is.** (Sí.) **No, it isn't.** (No.) **No, it is not.** (No.)
Is there a book on the table? (¿Hay un libro en la mesa?) **Yes, there is.** (Sí.) **No, there isn't.** (No, no hay.) **No, there is not.** (No, no hay.)	**Is your book on the table?** (¿Tu libro está en la mesa?) **Yes, it is.** (Sí.) **No, it isn't.** (No.) **No, it is not.** (No.)
Are there pizzas in the oven? (¿Hay pizzas en el horno?) **Yes, there are.** (Sí.) **No, there aren't.** (No, no hay.) **No, there are not.** (No, no hay.)	**Are the pizzas in the oven?** (¿Las pizzas están en el horno?) **Yes, they are.** (Sí.) **No, they aren't.** (No.) **No, they are not.** (No.)

Count and noncount nouns

Count nouns are nouns that can easily be counted. *Noncount nouns* are nouns that are singular but that cannot be preceded by **a** or **an**. For example, you say,

► **There isn't rice.** (No hay arroz.)

You don't say

► ~~There isn't a rice. (No hay un arroz.)~~

 **More Practice!**

P3.a Directions: Complete each sentence using **There is** or **There are**.

1. _There is_ _____ a meeting at the school.

2. _____ a party at Michele's house.

3. _____ many children at the park.

4. _____ six students from Haiti in my class.

5. _____ a restaurant next to my house.

6. _____ a sock under the couch.

P3.b Directions: Complete each sentence using **There** or **They're**.

1. _They're_ _____ at my sister's house.

2. _____ are pencils in your backpack.

3. _____ are many students from Mexico in my class.

4. _____ in the classroom.

5. _____ is a park across from her apartment.

6. _____ is cheese in the refrigerator.

P3.c Directions: Complete each sentence using **There** or **They**.

1. _They_ _____ are at work.

2. _____ are many people at the park.

3. _____ are my parents.

4. _____ are eggs in the refrigerador.

5. _____ are six years old.

6. _____ are plates (*plates*) in the sink.

P3.d Directions: In the first column write **Q** if the sentence is a *question* (*pregunta*) and **S** if the sentence is a *statement* (*declaración*). In the second column, put a period (.) or a question mark (?).

	Is this sentence a question or a statement?	Punctuation
1. Is there a cat under the sofa	1a. ___Q___	1b. _?_
2. Is there a park next to your house	2a. _____	2b. _____
3. There are four chairs in the kitchen	3a. _____	3b. _____
4. Is your house near your school	4a. _____	4b. _____
5. Is there a student from El Salvador in your class	5a. _____	5b. _____
6. Your brother is at my house now	6a. _____	6b. _____
7. Is there a backpack in your car	7a. _____	7b. _____

P3.e Directions: Read the paragraph and answer the questions. Use complete sentences. Use contractions when you can.

Chelsea is not happy. She is home from her job (*trabajo*) at the hospital. She is very hungry but (*pero*) there isn't food in the kitchen. There aren't apples on the table. There isn't rice or meat in the refrigerator. She also is thirsty but there isn't milk or soda. Then there is a noise (*ruido*). It is her husband, Andrew. He has two big bags (*bolsas*) of food (*comida*). He has fruit, rice, milk, meat and soda. Chelsea is very happy!

1. Is Chelsea hungry? _____Yes, she is._____

2. Are there apples on the table? _____

3. Is there rice in the refrigerator? _____

4. Is Chelsea married? _____

5. Are there clothes (*ropa*) in Andrew's bags? _____

5. Is there food in the bags? _____

6. Is Chelsea happy because she has food? _____

P3.f Directions: One of the sentences in each pair is not a correct sentence. Cross out the incorrect sentence.

1a. ~~There is a milk in the refrigerator.~~   1b. There is milk in the refrigerator.

2a. There is cheese on the table.   2b. There is a cheese on the table.

3a. There is many boys at the park.   3b. There are many boys at the park.

4a. There are meat in the kitchen.   4b. There is meat in the kitchen.

5a. There is a books on your dresser.   5b. There is a book on your dresser.

6a. There is an engineer in our class.   6b. There is a engineer in our class.

7a. There are three oranges in my backpack.   7b. There is three oranges in my backpack.

8a. There are many students in my class.   8b. There is many students in my class.

P3.g Directions: Translate these sentences. Use contractions when you can.

1. Hay un lápiz en mi mochila. _____There's a pencil in my backpack._____

2. Hay una manzana en la mesa. _____

3. Hay manzanas en la mesa. _____

4. Hay cuatro estudiantes de Perú en mi clase. _____

5. Hay dos sillas en la sala.. _____

6. Hay queso en el refrigerador. _____

7. Hay pizzas en el orno (*oven*). _____

8. Hay perros en el parque. _____

P3.h Directions: Write **count** or **noncount** next to each noun.

1. bread ___noncount___

2. boy _____

3. child _____

4. meat _____

5. juice _____

6. hat _____

7. money (*dinero*)_____

8. lamp _____

9. ice cream _____

10. milk _____

P3.i Directions: Look at the picture below. Then respond to each question using a long answer. Use a contraction when you can. Then, use one of the following short answers:

Yes, there is.   Yes, there are.

No, there isn't.   No, there aren't.

1. Is there a cat on the floor?

    1a. ___Yes, there's a cat on the floor.___

    1b. ___Yes, there is.___

2. Are there shoes under the counch?

    2a. _____

    2b. _____

3. Are there socks under the couch?

    3a. _____

    3b. _____

4. Is there a lamp on the table?

    4a. _____

    4b. _____

5. Are there two chairs in the living room?

    5a. _____

    5b. _____

6. Is there a window in the living room?

    6a. _____

    6b. _____

7. Is there a table in front of the couch?

    7a. _____

    7b. _____

Chapter 4

I play soccer once a week.

Verbs give language energy. They let you describe life's many activities. In this chapter, we focus on simple present tense verbs. You'll use these verbs to describe daily activities as well as to give information and express feelings and desires.

At the end of this chapter you will be able to

- identify verbs.
- spell simple present tense verbs.
- construct sentences that use simple present tense verbs to describe daily activities and express emotions and desires.
- know when to use simple present tense verbs.
- describe how often events occur.

work (trabajar)

eat (comer)

walk (caminar)

drive (manejar)

speak (hablar)

play (jugar)

A *verb* is a word that shows action; bailar, caminar, and nadar are all verbs. In both English and Spanish, every verb has a *tense* that tells whether it refers to something in the past, the present or the future. You can often tell the tense of the verb by the way it is spelled. Here are some examples of how the spelling of the Spanish verb corre changes depending on its tense:

Past tense	Juan corrió. Juan corría.
Simple present tense	Juan corre.
Future tense	Juan correrá.

Study the verbs on the left. Note that each one describes an action.

Other verbs are used to express facts, feelings, and desires. Here are some useful verbs that fit into this category:

Vocabulary: More verbs

| **live** (vivir) | **feel** *(sentir)* | **like** (gustar*)* | **have** (tener) |

All of the verbs defined on this page are the **base form** of the verb. The base form is sometimes called the **dictionary form** because it is the form of the verb that you'll find in the dictionary. You'll learn more about why the base form is important later in this chapter.

Grammar review: The verb to be

Remember that **am**, **is**, and **are** are also verbs. For more about using the verb **to be**, see Appendix B. More information is in *English Grammar: Step by Step 1*.

Grammar Review: Subjects and verbs

As you continue your study of verbs, it is important to be able to identify the **subject** and **verb** in a sentence.

► The *subject* of the sentence is usually the first noun or pronoun in the sentence. The subject tells you who or what the sentence is about.

► The *verb* tells you what action the subject performs.

Read this sentence:

► I play soccer on Tuesdays. (Juego al fútbol los martes.)

I is the subject because it tells who the sentence is about; **play** is the verb because it tells what action the subject, **I**, performs.

4.1.a Directions: Translate each verb into Spanish.

1. work trabajar
2. play
3. eat
4. live
5. speak

6. feel
7. wash
8. walk
9. drive
10. have

4.1.b Directions: Translate each verb into English.

1. manejar drive
2. trabajar
3. lavar
4. jugar
5. comer

6. gustar
7. vivir
8. tener
9. sentir
10. hablar

4.1.c Directions: Put one line under the subject. Put two lines under the verb.

1. Antonio walks to school.
2. Ana feels sad.
3. Lucas is from Mexico.
4. I speak English.
5. Jose and I are in love.
6. Joe and Ana play soccer at the park.
7. Andres and Lisa have a new baby.
8. Luis drives a beautiful car.
9. We like pizza.
10. They work at Bobos restaurant.
11. Paola speaks Chinese.
12. Ana feels tired.
13. I have two dogs.
14. Andres lives in Los Angeles.
15. Maria speaks Spanish.
16. Peter and James like Chinese food.

4.1.d Directions: Write **A** if the word is an adjective. Write **V** if the word is a verb. Write **N** if the word is a noun.

1. dog N
2. happy
3. tired
4. am
5. drive
6. short
7. Carlos
8. is

9. eat
10. bread
11. tall
12. school
13. live
14. are
15. New York
16. dresser

17. sofa
18. lamp
19. red
20. teacher
21. yellow
22. walk
23. fruit
24. have

4.1.e Directions: Cross out the one word in each line that is _not_ a verb.

1. am, speak, ~~bed~~
2. Andrew, live, feel

3. new, have, play
4. wash, is, ball

5. walk, car, drive
6. are, house, eat

In English there are two types of present tense verbs: ***simple present*** and ***present progressive.*** In this chapter and in Chapter 5 we'll talk about simple present verbs. In Chapter 6 we'll talk about present progressive verbs.

Consider the verb **eat** (comer). In Spanish, there are many forms of this verb in the simple present tense: como, comes, come, comemos, etc. In English there are only two forms: the base form, **eat**, and the "**s**" form, **eats**. Study this table:

When to use the base form	When to use the "s" form
I eat (yo como)	**he eats** (él come)
you eat (tú comes, usted come, ustedes comen)	**she eats** (ella come)
we eat (nosotros comemos, nosotras comemos)	**it eats**
they eat (ellos comen, ellas comen)	

Note the following:

▶ In the simple present tense, you use **eats** after **he**, **she** and **it**. You use the base form of the verb, **eat**, all other times.

This same rule applies to almost all simple present tense verbs; you use the base form followed by an **s** when you're referring to **he**, **she** or **it**. You use the base form all other times.

How do you write a sentence with a simple present tense verb? It's easy! Study this pattern:

Subject (noun or pronoun)	Simple present verb	Rest of sentence	Spanish translation
I	speak	English.	Hablo inglés.
She	speaks	English.	Ella habla inglés.

Here are more examples:

▶ I **drive** to work. (Manejo al trabajo.)
▶ We **get up** at 8:00. (Nos levantamos a las ocho.)
▶ He **plays** baseball at the park. (Él juega al béisbol en el parque.)

Caution! One of the most confusing parts of English grammar is that you add the letter **s** to the end of words for two completely different reasons.

▶ You add an **s** to a noun (a person, place, animal or thing) to make it plural. (For example, **books** is the plural of **book**.)
▶ You add an **s** to the base form of a present tense verb when the subject of the sentence is **he**, **she** or **it**. (**He lives** in Guatemala.)

In addition, many words in English end in **s**. For example, **dress** (vestido), **kiss** (beso), **his** (su de él), and many more.

4.2.a Directions: Complete the sentence using work or works.

1. I ___work___ at Bobos Restaurant.
2. He _____ at Bobos Restaurant.
3. We _____ at Bobos Restaurant.
4. You _____ at Bobos Restaurant.
5. She _____ at Bobos Restaurant.
6. They _____ at Bobos Restaurant.

4.2.b Directions: Complete the sentence using live or lives.

1. He ___lives___ in New York.
2. You _____ in Chicago.
3. We _____ in Los Angeles.
4. They _____ in Mexico.
5. I _____ in Honduras.
6. She _____ in El Salvador.

4.2.c Directions: Complete the sentence using like or likes.

1. We ___like___ pizza.
2. You _____ milk.
3. They _____ cheese.
4. I _____ soccer.
5. He _____ the United States.
6. She _____ her class.

4.2.d Directions: Underline the correct verb in each sentence.

1. I (play, plays) soccer.
2. He (live, lives) in a big house.
3. You (eat, eats) meat every day.
4. I (speak, speaks) Spanish.
5. We (work, works) in Chicago.
6. You (live, lives) in a big city.
7. They (walk, walks) to school.
8. I (eat, eats) lunch at 2:00.
9. She (speak, speaks) English.
10. She (work, works) at a school.
11. They (play, plays) golf.
12. I (like, likes) fruit.
13. She (live, lives) in Sonora.
14. She (eat, eats) ice cream at school.
15. I (feel, feels) tired.
16. He (drive, drives) her car.
17. She (feel, feels) sick today.
18. You (walk, walks) every day.

4.2.e Directions: One of the sentences in each pair is not a correct sentence. Cross out the incorrect sentence.

1a. I play soccer.
2a. He live in a big house.
3a. I like watermelon (*sandía*).
4a. He feel sad.
5a. We work in Chicago.
6a. You walk to school.
7a. She plays tennis.
8a. I walks in the park.
9a. They work at a restaurant.

1b. ~~I plays soccer.~~
2b. He lives in a big house.
3b. I likes watermelon.
4b. He feels sad.
5b. We works in Chicago.
6b. You walks to school.
7b. She play tennis.
8b. I walk in the park.
9b. They works at a restaurant.

More about Simple Present Tense Verbs

You now know how to use the simple present tense when the subject of a sentence is a pronoun such as **I**, **you**, **he**, **she**, **it**, **we** or **they**. But suppose the subject of the sentence is a noun such as **Carlos** or **Barack and Michelle**? Study these examples:

I **live** in that house.
(Vivo en esa casa.)

Gabriela **lives** in that house.
(Gabriela vive en esa casa.)

Notice the following:

► In the first sentence, the subject of the sentence is **I**, so you use the base form of the verb, which is **live**.
► In the second sentence, the subject of the sentence is **Gabriela**, so you use the **s** form of the verb, which is **lives**.

The following table summarizes how to form simple present tense verbs.

Add **s** to the base form of the verb to refer to **he**, **she**, **it**, one male, one female, or one thing.	Use the base form of the verb all other times.
Luis lives in Boston. (Luis vive en Boston.) **Laura lives in Boston.** (Laura vive en Boston.) **My brother lives in Boston.** (Mi hermano vive en Boston.) **She lives in Boston.** (Ella vive en Boston.)	**I live in Boston.** (Yo vivo en Boston.) **My friends live in Boston.** (Mis amigos viven en Boston.) **They live in Boston.** (Ellos viven en Boston.) **Ana and I live in Boston.** (Ana y yo vivimos en Boston.)

Grammar Review: To use the simple present tense correctly, you'll need to make sure you know the following irregular plural nouns:

Singular noun	Irregular plural noun
man (hombre)	**men** (hombres)
woman (mujer)	**women** (mujeres)
child (niño)	**children** (niños)
person (persona)	**people** (personas)
foot (pie)	**feet** (pies)
tooth (diente)	**teeth** (dientes)

4.3.a Directions: Write the subject pronoun—**he**, **she**, **it**, **we** or **they**—that you can substitute for each noun or nouns.

1. Lucas ___he___
2. Ana _____
3. the students _____
4. The woman _____
5. The people _____
6. My teacher and I _____

7. the book _____
8. Henry and I _____
9. Peter _____
10. The school _____
11. The flowers _____
12. Charles and Bryan _____

4.3.b Directions: Complete the sentence using **live** or **lives**.

1. Angela ___lives___ in New York.
2. Luis _____ in Chicago.
3. My cousins _____ in New York.

4. I _____ in Michoacan.
5. Edgar and I _____ in Honduras.
6. The teacher _____ in an apartment.

4.3.c. Directions: Complete the sentence using **like** or **likes**.

1. Andrew ___likes___ apples.
2. Laura _____ expensive cars.
3. My sisters and I _____ New York.

4. Anna _____ flowers.
5. Bruce and Elizabeth _____ cheese.
6. The teacher _____ her students.

4.3.d. Directions: Complete the sentence using **speak** or **speaks**.

1. Francisco ___speaks___ English.
2. Dan _____ Spanish.
3. My parents _____ English.

4. The students _____ French.
5. I _____ English.
6. Emily _____ Spanish and French.

4.3.e. Directions: Underline the correct verb in each sentence.

1. Juan (play, <u>plays</u>) soccer.
2. Anna and Lucas (live, lives) in an old house.
3. The children (eat, eats) tacos for lunch.
4. Omar (feel, feels) sad.
5. Patricia (work, works) at a restaurant.

6. The man (play, plays) golf.
7. We (like, likes) rice.
8. I (feel, feels) tired.
9. The women (work, works) at a school.
10. My sister (play, plays) tennis.

4.3.f. Directions: Translate each sentence.

1. Los estudiantes viven en Hawaii.   The students live in Hawaii.

2. Mi mamá se siente feliz.   _____

3. Camino en el parque.   _____

4. Marian y Marcos viven en Guadalajara.   _____

5. Lisa trabaja en Fries Restaurant.   _____

4.4 Using Simple Present Tense Verbs Correctly

Using the simple present tense correctly is one of the most challenging aspects of learning to speak and write English. This section illustrates some of the common errors non-English speakers make when using simple present tense verbs, and then explains how to avoid them.

Adding the verb **to be** to simple present tense verbs

Many people learning English incorrectly place a form of the verb **to be** (**is**, **am** or **are**) before the simple present tense verb. Study these examples of correct and incorrect sentences.

Correct sentences	Incorrect sentences
Juan lives in Miami. (Juan vive en Miami.)	~~Juan is live in Miami.~~
I speak English. (Hablo inglés.)	~~I am speak English.~~
Chelsea and I run in the park. (Chelsea y yo corremos en el parque.)	~~Chelsea and I are run in the park.~~

A form of the verb **to be** is used with present progressive verbs. For example, it is correct to say, **He is playing soccer**. You'll learn about present progressive verbs in Chapter 6.

Adding **ing** to simple present tense verbs

Another common mistake people learning English make is to add **ing** to the base verb. This is not correct. Study these examples.

Correct sentences	Incorrect sentences
Juan lives in Miami. (Juan vive en Miami.)	**Juan ~~living~~ in Miami.**
I speak English. (Hablo inglés.)	**I ~~speaking~~ English.**
Gaby and I run in the park. (Gaby y yo corremos en el parque.)	**Gaby and I ~~running~~ in the park.**

It is correct to add **ing** to the base verb of the verb when you are using the present progressive tense. Thus, it is correct to say, **He is studying now**. You'll learn about present progressive verbs in Chapter 6.

4.4.a Directions: One of the sentences in each line is not correct. Cross out the incorrect sentence.

1a. ~~I am study English.~~	1b. I study English.
2a. They are like the United States.	2b. They like the United States.
3a. Susan she is likes soccer.	3b. Susan likes soccer.
4a. I drive to work.	4b. I am driver to work.
5a. You work today.	5b. You are work today.
6a. I feel sad.	6b. I feeling sad.
7a. I play volleyball with my friends.	7b. I playing volleyball with my friends.
8a. I driving to work.	8b. I drive to work.
9a. I having two jobs.	9b. I have two jobs.
10a. My friend is lives in Chicago.	10b. My friend lives in Chicago.

4.4.b Directions: Underline the correct verb in each sentence.

1. Juan (is play, <u>plays</u>) with his brother.
2. We (live, living) in an old house.
3. Andrew and I (are eat, eat) meat for lunch.
4. Stuart (feels, is feels) tired because he is sick.
5. Alonso (speaks, speaking) English at home.
6. You (live, living) in an apartment.
7. The child (walk, walks) to school.
8. I (drive, driver) an old car.
9. The man (play, plays) golf.
10. We (like, likes) oranges.
11. I (am like, like) milk.
12. The boys (work, works) at a school in New Haven.
13. I (play, am play) tennis.
14. The woman (is drive, drives) to work.
15. The girls (play, plays) with their toys.
16. The teachers (feel, they feel) lazy today.

4.4.c Directions: Each sentence contains an error. The error is underlined. Rewrite each sentence so that it is correct. Every sentence should use the simple present tense.

1. The engineers <u>working</u> eight hours a day.　The engineers work eight hours a day.

2. I <u>going to</u> class at 2:00.

3. The children <u>watching</u> television at 3:30.

4. I <u>am study</u> in the kitchen.

5. Ernesto <u>is work</u> at a restaurant.

6. I <u>am have</u> two sisters.

7. We <u>are like</u> Chinese food.

8. Ana <u>feel</u> sick today.

9. We <u>lives</u> in Seattle.

10. I <u>am eat</u> breakfast at work.

English Grammar: Step by Step 2

Rules for Spelling Simple Present Tense Verbs

When the subject of a sentence is **he, she, it,** or one male, female or thing, you add an **s** to the base verb. This rule applies most of the time. But there are a few other spelling rules you'll also need to learn. This section explains them.

When to add **es** instead of **s** to a simple present tense verb

If a base verb ends in **s, ss, ch, sh, x** or **z**, add **es** instead of **s** to the base verb. Here are some examples:

► He **watches** television. (Él mira televisión.)

► Lucy **brushes** her teeth in the morning. (Lucy se cepilla los dientes en la mañana.)

► Jose **relaxes** on Sundays. (José se relaja los domingos.)

In the first example, the base form of the verb is **watch** (mirar). Because **watch** ends in **ch,** you add **es** instead of **s** to the base form of the verb. In the second example, the base form of the verb is **brush** (cepillar). Because **brush** ends in **sh,** you add **es** instead of **s**. In the third example, the base form of the verb is **relax** (relajar). Because **relax** ends in **x** you add **es** instead of **s**.

When to drop the **y** and add **ies** to a simple present tense verb

If the base form of the verb ends in a **y** preceded by a consonant, delete the **y** and add **ies** to the base verb. (Remember that in English the consonants are **b, c,** d, **f, g,** h, **j, k, l, m, n, p, q, r,** s, t, v, **w, x, y** and **z**. The vowels are **a, e, i, o** and **u.**)

Here are some examples that illustrate dropping the **y** and adding **ies** to the base verb.

► Lisa **studies** English. (Lisa estudia inglés.)

► Lisa **carries** her books to class. (Lisa carga sus libros a clase.)

In the first example, the base form of the verb is **study** (estudiar). This verb ends in a **y** preceded by the consonant **d,** so you change the **y** to **i** and add **es**. In the second example, the base form of the verb is **carry** (cargar). This verb ends in a **y** preceded by the consonant **r,** so you change the **y** to **i** and add **es**.

If a verb ends in a **y** preceded by a vowel, you simply add **s** to the base form of the verb. Here are some examples:

► She **plays** soccer at her school. (Ella juega al fútbol en su escuela.)

► Sam **pays** the cashier. (Sam le paga a la cajera.)

4.5.a Directions: Complete with the correct "s" form of the verb.

Base form	"s" form	Base form	"s" form
1. fix	fixes	7. brush	
2. watch		8. write (*escribir*)	
3. study		9. carry	
4. relax		10. feel	
5. speak		11. play	
6. pay (*pagar*)		12. listen (*escuchar*)	

4.5.b Directions: Choose the correct word from the box. Use each word once.

watch	brush	play	drive	carry	study
watches	brushes	have	drives	carries	studies

1. Pedro _____carries_____ his books in his backpack.
2. I _____ English at Buena Vista Community College.
3. My mother _____ television at night.
4. We _____ volleyball in the park on Sundays.
5. The children _____ television in the afternoon.
6. The engineer _____ mathematics at the university.
7. I _____ my hair in the morning.
8. I _____ home from work at 6 p.m.
9. Josephina _____ to work at 8 a.m.
10. My aunt and uncle _____ five children.
11. Alma _____ her daughter's hair.
12. I _____ my backpack to school.

4.5.c Directions: Cross out the word that is <u>not</u> a verb.

1. ~~good,~~ listen, work

2. cheap, play, pay

3. has, goes, hospital

4. is, hair (*pelo,*) brush

5. are, relax, ball

6. English, write, study

7. car, drives, drive

8. carries, watches, happy

Irregular Simple Present Tense Verbs: *Goes, Does* and *Has*

In both English and Spanish, there are two types of verbs: ***regular verbs*** and ***irregular verbs***. *Regular verbs* are verbs whose spelling is based on rules. *Irregular verbs* are verbs whose spelling can't be predicted. The good news is that there are many fewer irregular verbs in English than in Spanish!

You already know one irregular English verb: **to be** (**am**, **is** and **are**). All of the other English simple present tense verbs that you have studied so far are regular verbs; their spelling follows definite rules. In this section, you will learn about three verbs that are irregular in the simple present tense: **go** (ir), **do** (hacer) and **have** (tener). Study this conversation:

I **have** two children.
(Tengo dos niños.)

My sister **has** four children.
(Mi hermana tiene cuatro niños.)

Note that in the second sentence, the verb is **has** not ~~**haves**~~.

Here is how to conjugate the three verbs that are irregular in the present tense:

	have (tener)*	**go** (ir)	**do** (hacer)**
Base form	I have	I go	I do
	You have	You go	You do
	We have	We go	We do
	They have	They go	They do
"s" form	He has	He goes	He does
	She has	She goes	She does
	It has	It goes	It does

Notice the following:

▶ **have** changes to **has**.
▶ **go** changes to **goes**.
▶ **do** changes to **does**.

* See *English Grammar: Step by Step 1* for more about how to use **have** and **has**.

** The Spanish verb hacer has two meanings in English: **do** and **make**. Do is also used when asking questions and making negative statements in the simple present tense. In these cases **do** doesn't mean hacer at all! You'll learn more about this verb in Chapter 5.

4.6.a Directions: Complete the sentence using **have** or **has**.

1. I __have__ a job.
2. He _____ many friends.
3. Cecilia _____ an old car.
4. That man _____ a big problem.
5. The boy _____ a new toy.

6. You _____ a problem.
7. Louisa _____ a good mother.
8. They _____ a new baby.
9. Dulce and Paul _____ three children.
10. We _____ an expensive apartment.

4.6.b Directions: Complete the sentence using **go** or **goes**.

1. We __go__ to school at 8:00.
2. Lisa _____ to work at 3:30.
3. I _____ home after work.
4. Meg _____ to church on Sunday.
5. They _____ to the park once a week.

6. You often _____ to the doctor.
7. The students _____ to school late.
8. The man _____ to work in the afternoon.
9. The women _____ to Los Angeles.
10. Luis and Edgar _____ home at 5:00.

4.6.c Directions: Complete with the correct form of the verb.

Base form	"s" form	Base form	"s" form
1. speak	speaks	7. write	
2. go		8. do	
3. study		9. work	
4. have		10. relax	
5. watch		11. read (*leer*)	
6. listen		12. fix	

4.6.d Directions: Rewrite this story so that it is about Ana Banks. The first two sentences are done for you.

My name is Ana Banks. I live in Los Angeles. I have a job. I work at Celia's Restaurant. I am a cashier. I like my job. I drive to my job. I also study English. My class is on Tuesday and Thursday from 7 p.m. to 9 p.m.

Her name is Ana Banks. She lives in Los Angeles.

_____

_____

_____

_____

You use simple present verbs for two main purposes: to talk about habits, customs and schedules, and to talk about facts, feelings and desires.

Simple present tense verbs for habits, customs and schedules

You often use simple present verbs to talk about activities you do as part of your daily routine. Read Hector's daily schedule. The verb is underlined.

7:00 **get up** (levantarse)	1:00 **eat** lunch (almorzar)
7:15 **take** a shower (ducharse)	5:00 **finish** work and **go** home (terminar el trabajo e ir a la casa)
7:45 **eat** breakfast (desayunar)	5:15 **study** English (estudiar inglés)
8:00 **drive** to work (manejar al trabajo)	6:30 **eat** dinner (cenar)
8:30 **start** work (empezar a trabajar)	7:00 **watch** television (mirar televisión)
10:30 **take** a break (tomar un descanso)	10:00 **sleep** (dormir), **go** to bed (acostarse)

Notice the following:

▶ Some English verbs consist of more than one word. **get up** is one of these verbs.

▶ There are no English verbs for desayunar, almorzar and cenar. Instead you say **eat breakfast**, **eat lunch** and **eat dinner**.

To describe Hector's schedule, you might say things like this:

▶ Hector **gets up** at 7:00. (Héctor se levanta a las siete.)

▶ He **takes** a shower at 7:15. (Se ducha a las siete y cuarto.)

To talk about your schedule, as opposed to Hector's schedule, you might say

▶ I **get up** at 7:00. (Me levanto a las siete.)

▶ I **take** a shower at 7:15. (Me ducho a las siete y cuarto.)

Do you know why you add **s** to verbs in the first two sentences above but use the base form of the verb in the second two sentences?

Simple present tense verbs for facts, feelings and desires

You also use simple present tense verbs in sentences that talk about facts, feelings and desires. The verbs below are used for this purpose. Study the following sentences to see how these verbs are used.

▶ Ariana **needs** a job. (Ariana necesita un trabajo.)
▶ I **know** your sister. (Yo conozco a tu hermana.)
▶ She **knows** your name. (Ella sabe tu nombre.)
▶ Alison **wants** a dog. (Alison quiere un perro.)

4.7.a Directions: Emma Medina is a secretary. Read her schedule. Then write a sentence about what she does at each of the times listed below.

6:00 a.m.: get up	7:00 a.m.: walk to work	4:00 p.m.: watch television	7:00 p.m.: go to class
6:10 a.m.: take a shower	11:30 a.m.: eat lunch	5:30 p.m.: prepare dinner	9:30 p.m.: go home
6:20 a.m.: eat breakfast	3:30 p.m.: walk home	6:00: p.m.: eat dinner	10:30 p.m.: go to bed

1. (6:00 a.m.)   She gets up at 6:00 a.m.

2. (6:10 a.m.)

3. (6:20 a.m.)

4. (7:00 a.m.)

5. (11:30 a.m.)

6. (4:00 p.m.)

7. (5:30 p.m.)

8. (7:00 p.m.)

9. (10:30 p.m.)

4.7.b Directions: Put a check (√) next to the sentences that are true for you.
1. _____ I take a shower every day. (*todos los días*)
2. _____ I eat breakfast every day.
3. _____ I eat lunch every day.
4. _____ I eat dinner every day.
5. _____ I watch television every day.
6. _____ I speak English every day.
7. _____ I clean (*limpio*) my house every day.
8. _____ I sleep eight hours every night.

4.7.c Directions: Read the story. Then answer each question with **T** for **True** or **F** for **False**.

My name is Mario Hernandez. I am a painter (*pintor*). I work five days a week. I work from Monday to Friday. I work from 9:00 a.m. to 3:00 p.m. I go to sleep at 11:15. I go to English class on Monday, Tuesday, and Thursday evenings. I need to study English. On Wednesday evenings I play soccer at Central Park. On Friday evening I relax. I am tired.

1. Mario works seven days a week.   F

2. Mario plays soccer at Central Park.

3. Mario is a cook.

4. Mario relaxes on Friday evenings.

5. Mario starts (*empieza*) work at 9:00 p.m.

6. Mario plays soccer on Wednesday evenings.

Adverbs of Frequency: *Always, Usually, Sometimes, Never*

You often use simple present verbs to tell how often you do something. Read this conversation:

My husband <u>always</u> watches TV. He <u>never</u> cleans the house.
(Mi esposo siempre mira televisión. Nunca limpia la casa.)

Always and **never** are called *adverbs of frequency*. An *adverb* is a part of speech that modifies a verb, an adjective or another adverb. *Adverbs of frequency* modify verbs by telling how often an action is performed. Study these adverbs of frequency.

Vocabulary: Adverbs of frequency			
always (siempre)	**usually** (normalmente)	**sometimes** (a veces, algunas veces)	**never** (nunca)

Here is the pattern for sentences that include adverbs of frequency. Notice that you place the adverb of frequency <u>after</u> the subject.

Subject	Adverb of frequency	Simple present verb	Rest of sentence	Spanish translation
I	sometimes	eat	breakfast.	A veces desayuno.

Here are more examples. Here again, notice that the adverb is placed after the subject.

► We **never** walk to school. (Nunca caminamos a la escuela.)

► Mario **always** brushes his teeth in the morning. (Mario siempre se cepilla los dientes por la mañana.)

► They **usually** eat dinner at 8:00. (Ellos normalmente cenan a las 8:00.)

4.8.a Directions: Rewrite the sentence using the adverb of frequency in parentheses. Remember that you place the adverb of frequency after the subject.

1. (often) I drink milk.   I often drink milk.
2. (always) I watch TV.
3. (sometimes) I play soccer.
4. (usually) I eat meat for dinner.
5. (never) My boss speaks English.
6. (usually) My teacher speaks English.
7. (never) Amanda's husband drives to work.
8. (often) We listen to (*escuchamos*) music.
9. (never) My parents eat Chinese food.
10. (sometimes) The students walk to school.

4.8.b Directions: Write sentences that tell how often you do each of the following activities. Tell the truth. Use always, usually, sometimes or never.

1. read the newspaper
2. play soccer
3. watch television
4. eat breakfast
5. eat lunch
6. go to the park
7. go to church
8. go to the beach

4.8.c Directions: One of the sentences in each pair is not a correct sentence. Cross out the incorrect sentence.

1a. I never play soccer.   1b. ~~I play soccer never.~~
2a. I usually take a shower at night.   2b. I take a shower at night usually.
3a. My sister does always her homework.   3b. My sister always does her homework.
4a. Louisa cooks sometimes dinner.   4b. Louisa sometimes cooks dinner.
5a. My sister studies sometimes English.   5b. My sister sometimes studies English.
6a. My daughter walks always to school.   6b. My daughter always walks to school.
7a. Luke usually eats dinner at home.   7b. Luke eats dinner usually at home.
8a. The boys play soccer never on the weekends.   8b. The boys never play soccer on the weekends.
9a. I feel tired always after work.   9b. I always feel tired after work.
10a. My dog usually sleeps on my bed.   10b. My dog sleeps on my bed usually.

Once a week, once a month, once a year

The adverbs of frequency you learned about in the last section—**never**, **sometimes**, **usually** and **always**—give you a general idea of how often an event occurs. But suppose you want to be more specific. To do that, you'll need to learn a few more phrases. Study this conversation between two friends.

Now study this vocabulary:

Vocabulary: Adverb phrases	
every week (cada semana, todas las semanas) **once a week** (una vez por semana)	**twice a week** (dos veces por semana)
three times a week (tres veces por semana)	**four times a week** (cuatro veces por semana)

Note the following:

> ▶ As you see from the chart above, when you do something one time you use the word **once** and when you do something two times you use the word **twice**. After that, you just say **three times**, **four times**, **five times**, etc.

> ▶ Even though **once** is the same as the word for eleven in Spanish, you pronounce it differently. The English pronunciation is uónc.

Here's the pattern:

Subject	Simple present verb	Rest of sentence	Adverb phrase	Spanish translation
I	play	soccer	twice a week.	Juego al fútbol dos veces por semana.

Study the following examples. Notice that the adverb phrase always is placed at the end of the sentence.

> ▶ I visit my aunt **twice a month**. (Visito a mi tía dos veces por mes.)

> ▶ Her parents go to Peru **four times a year**. (Sus padres van a Perú cuatro veces por año.)

4.9.a Directions: Rewrite the sentence using the time expression in parentheses. Remember that you place these time expressions at the end of the sentence.

1. (once a week) I drink soda.   I drink soda once a week.

2. (five days a week) Lionel watches TV.

3. (every day) Luke plays volleyball.

4. (five days a week) Peter does his homework.

5. (every day) The students go to the library.

6. (three times a week) Magali goes to church.

7. (twice a month) The children eat pizza.

8. (once a year) I go to the beach.

4.9.b Directions: Write sentences that tell how often you do each of the following activities. Tell the truth. Use once a day, twice a day, once a week, etc.

1. take a shower (*ducharse*)

2. use the computer

3. read the newspaper

4. call my country

5. play soccer

6. eat out (*comer afuera*)

4.9.c Directions: One of the sentences in each pair is not a correct sentence. Cross out the incorrect sentence.

1a. I brush my teeth twice a day.   1b. ~~I brush twice a day my teeth.~~

2a. I call my family once a week.   2b. I call once a week my family.

3a. We work five days a week.   3b. We five days a week work.

4a. The students go to the library five day a week.   4b. The students go to the library five days a week.

5a. My aunt and uncle every year visit Mexico.   5b. My aunt and uncle visit Mexico every year.

4.9.d Directions: Translate these sentences.

1. Trabajo cinco días por semana.   I work five days a week.

2. Lucas trabaja seis días por semana.

3. Voy a Dallas una vez por semana.

4. Mi tío va a Los Angeles una vez por mes.

5. Ernesto visita México dos veces por año.

A *verb* is a word that shows action. Examples are **dance** (bailar) and **walk** (caminar). Verbs are also used to express facts, feelings and desires. Examples are **feel** (sentir) and **live** (vivir). **Am**, **is**, and **are** also are verbs.

Simple present tense verbs

Simple present tense verbs are used to talk about habits, customs and schedules and facts, feelings and desires. Sentences with simple present tense verbs have this pattern:

Subject (noun or pronoun)	Simple present verb	Rest of sentence	Spanish translation
I	speak	English.	Hablo inglés.
Juan	speaks	English	Juan habla inglés.

To form simple present tense verbs, you usually follow these rules:

Add **s** to the base form of the verb to refer to **he, she, it,** one male, one female, or one thing.	Use the base form of the verb all other times.
Luis lives in Boston. (Luis vive en Boston.)	**I live in Boston.** (Yo vivo en Boston.)
Laura lives in Boston. (Laura vive en Boston.)	**My friends live in Boston.** (Mis amigos viven en Boston.)
My brother lives in Boston. (Mi hermano vive en Boston.)	**They live in Boston.** (Ellos viven en Boston.)

When the subject of a sentence is **he**, **she**, **it** or one male, female or thing, you usually add an **s** to the base verb.

▶ **live** → **lives**

If a base verb ends in **s**, **ss**, **ch**, **sh**, **x** or **z**, add **es** instead of **s** to the base verb.

▶ **watch** → **watches**

If the base form of the verb ends in a **y** preceded by a consonant, delete the **y** and add i**es** to the base verb.

▶ **carry** → **carries**

The following are irregular present tense verbs:

have changes to **has**.   **do** changes to **does**.   **go** changes to **goes**.

Adverbs of frequency

Adverbs of frequency tell how often something occurs. Some adverbs of frequency are **always** (siempre), **usually** (normalmente), **sometimes** (a veces, algunas veces) and **never** (nunca). You place the adverb of frequency after the subject.

Subject	Adverb of frequency	Simple present verb	Rest of sentence	Spanish translation
I	sometimes	eat	breakfast.	A veces desayuno.

You also use phrases like **once a week, once a month, twice a month,** etc. to tell how often events occur. Those sentences have this pattern:

Subject	Simple present verb	Rest of sentence	Adverb phrase	Spanish translation
I	play	soccer	twice a week.	Juego al fútbol dos veces por semana.

 **More Practice!**

P4.a Directions: Write **A** if the word is an adjective. Write **V** if the word is a verb. Write **N** if the word is a noun.

1. cat	N	9. cheap		17. bedroom	
2. thin		10. talk		18. hat	
3. healthy		11. green		19. late	
4. study		12. like		20. aunt	
5. blouse		13. feel		21. backpack	
6. handsome		14. shoes		22. am	
7. Alex		15. Florida		23. go	
8. shirt		16. has		24. have	

P4.b Directions: Underline the correct verb in each sentence.

1. I (<u>work</u>, works) late on Mondays.
2. He (live, lives) in San Francisco.
3. They (like, likes) apples.
4. I (speak, speaks) English.
5. The children (play, plays) at the park.
6. Alma (have, has) three children.
7. The students (go, goes) to school at 9:00.
8. I (eat, eats) pizza every day.
9. Alex (finish, finishes) (*terminar*) class at 10:00.
10. Laura never (watch, watches) television.
11. My parents (live, lives) in Japan.
12. I (brush, brushes) my hair every morning.
13. The students always (study, studies) in the library.
14. The cook (work, works) six days a week.
15. Chelsea (take, takes) a break at 5:00.
16. They usually (drive, drives) to work.
17. I (like, likes) telenovelas.
18. She (take, takes) a shower in the morning.
19. The men (eat, eats) tacos for lunch every day.
20. My daughter (feel, feels) sick.
21. He (drive, drives) a big car.
22. Lucas and Ana often (go, goes) to bed late.
23. Warren (need, needs) (*necesitar*) money.
24. Sharon and Frank (study, studies) Italian.
25. I never (work, works) on Sunday.
26. The doctors always (eat, eats) lunch at the hospital.
27. Mrs. Marshall (have, has) a new car.
28. They always (go, goes) to church on Sunday.

P4.c Directions: Complete with the correct "**s**" form of the verb.

Base form	"**s**" form	Base form	"**s**" form
1. speak	speaks	8. write	
2. brush		9. finish	
3. have		10. read	
4. fix		11. do	
5. carry		12. take	
6. relax		13. feel	
7. study		14. make	

P4.d Directions: Rewrite this story so that it is about Liliana Garcia.

My name is Liliana Garcia. I live in Dallas, Texas. I am a student. I study English and math. I go to Mathews Community College. I also have a job. I am an engineer. I work in a large office. I fix computers. I like my job.

Her name is Liliana Garcia. She lives in Dallas, Texas. _____

_____

_____

_____

P4.e Directions: Read the story. Then write **T** for **True** (Verdadero) or **F** for **False** (Falso) next to each sentence.

My name is Ellen. I usually get up at 7:00. Then, I take a shower and eat breakfast at home. I drive to work. I am a secretary. My job is 45 minutes from my house. I work from Monday to Friday. I work from 9:00 a.m. to 5:00 p.m. I get home from work about 6:00. Then I go to the gym for an hour. When I return home I am very hungry. I have a roommate (*compañera de cuarto*). Her name is Aline. Aline usually makes dinner. She is a very good cook. After dinner, I watch TV for an hour and go to bed. I am always very tired.

I like the weekends (*fines de semana*) . I sleep late on Saturday. I usually go dancing on Saturday night. On Sunday I relax, clean my house and buy food. I always go to bed early on Sunday night.

1. Ellen gets up at 7:30.   F _____
2. Ellen eats breakfast at her house.   _____
3. Ellen walks to work.   _____
4. Ellen works five days a week.   _____
5. Ellen goes to the gym before work.   _____
6. Ellen makes dinner every night.   _____
7. Aline is Ellen's roommate.   _____
8. Ellen watches TV after dinner.   _____
9. Ellen works on the weekends.   _____
10. Ellen goes to the movies on Saturday night. _____
11. Ellen cleans her house on Sunday.   _____
12. Ellen goes to bed late on Sunday night.   _____

P4.f Directions: One of the sentences in each pair is not a correct sentence. Cross out the incorrect sentence.

1a. I like soccer.	1b. ~~I likes soccer.~~
2a. I need a job.	2b. I needs a job.
3a. Angela like watermelon.	3b. Angela likes watermelon.
4a. Our living room haves two sofas.	4b. Our living room has two sofas.
5a. My sister study English two nights a week.	5b. My sister studies English two nights a week.
6a. My daughter walk to school.	6b. My daughter walks to school.

7a. The boys play tennis twice a week.

7b. The boys plays tennis twice a week.

8a. Julio study English at home.

8b. Julio studies English at home.

P4.g Directions: Rewrite the sentence using the time expression in parentheses. Remember that you place these time expressions at the end of the sentence.

1. (once a week) I drink coffee.

    I drink coffee once a week.

2. (twice a month) Pat goes to the gym.

3. (six days a week) Phyillis works.

4. (twice a week) I wash clothes (*lavar la ropa*).

5. (once a month) The students go to the museum (*al museo*).

6. (twice a year) Leo goes to the beach.

P4.h Directions: Write sentences that tell how often you do each of the following activities. Tell the truth. Use always, usually, sometimes, or never.

1. use a computer

2. sing (*cantar*) in the shower

3. visit my country

4. drink (*beber*) milk

5. eat Chinese food

6. play soccer

7. call (*llamar*) my family

8. go to English class

P4.i Directions: Translate these sentences.

1. Nunca voy a San Francisco.

    I never go to San Francisco.

2. Siempre tomo café por la mañana.

3. Mi hija tiene dos trabajos.

4. Ana lava su ropa una vez por semana.

5. Mi madre va a Chicago dos veces por año.

6. Trabajo cinco días por semana.

7. Mi jefe siempre habla inglés.

8. Los estudiantes normalmente caminan a la escuela.

Chapter 5

I don't have a car.

Yﾞou have learned how to use simple present tense verbs to talk about what you do every day. In this chapter you'll learn to use those same verbs to talk about what you don't do. You'll also learn to ask and answer questions about where, what time and when activities take place. For example, you'll learn how to ask people where they live, what time they work, when they study and lots more. And, of course, you'll also learn how to answer these questions!

At the end of this chapter you will be able to

- use simple present tense verbs in negative sentences.
- ask and answer questions about where, what time and when activities take place.

5.1 Negative Statements with Present Tense Verbs

In the last chapter, you learned about affirmative statements with simple present tense verbs. In this chapter, you'll learn about negative statements with simple present tense verbs. Read this conversation:

Notice the following:

- ▶ The first sentence is affirmative and the second sentence is negative.

- ▶ In the affirmative sentence, the subject is **you** so you use the base form of the verb, **need**.

- ▶ In the negative sentence, the first verb is **do**. (**Do** is called an *auxiliary verb* or *helping verb*, that is, a verb that helps the main verb.) The second verb, **need**, is the *base form* of the main verb.

English vs. Spanish: Many people learning English try to translate **do not** when it is used in negative sentences. Don't even try! There is no translation. Note that when **do** is used in a negative sentence it does not mean hacer.

Grammar Recipe: To make a negative statement in the present tense when the subject is **I**, **we**, **you** or **they**, place **do not** immediately before the base form of the verb.

Here's the pattern:

Subject	do not	Simple present verb	Rest of sentence	Spanish translation
I	do not	speak	English.	No hablo inglés.

Here are some examples of affirmative and negative sentences with simple present tense verbs.

Affirmative sentences	Negative sentences
I have a car. (Tengo carro.)	**I <u>do not</u> have a car.** (No tengo carro.)
We work at Rick's Restaurant. (Trabajamos en Ricks Restaurant.)	**We <u>do not</u> work at Rick's Restaurant.** (No trabajamos en Ricks Restaurant.)
The students speak Spanish. (Los estudiantes hablan español.)	**The students <u>do not</u> speak Spanish.** (Los estudiantes no hablan español.)

5.1.a Directions: Write **A** if the statement is affirmative and **N** if the statement is negative.

1. I do not have a job. __N__
2. We live in New Jersey. _____
3. The children do not like pizza. _____
4. I feel tired. _____
5. My parents do not have a car. _____

6. I need a job. _____
7. My daughter needs a new dress. _____
8. The students do not study every day. _____
9. The cooks do not work on Saturday. _____
10. We do not drive to work. _____

5.1.b Directions: Make each affirmative sentence negative using **do not**.

1. I have a big family.   I do not have a big family.
2. I have a job.
3. I need a job.
4. I like your shirt.
5. The women work on Tuesdays.
6. The children play soccer once a week.
7. They study English at the university.
8. We get up early (*temprano*).

5.1.c Directions: Translate each sentence.

1. No tengo una casa grande.   I do not have a big house.
2. No hablo inglés.
3. No estudio español.
4. No hablas italiano (*Italian*).
5. No necesitamos un sofá nuevo.
6. Ella no camina a la escuela.
7. Ellos no viven en Los Angeles.

5.1.d Directions: One of the sentences in each line is not correct. Cross out the incorrect sentence.

1a. ~~I no have a job.~~
2a. They do not work at Bo's Restaurant.
3a. We no like Chinese food.
4a. I not work on the weekends.
5a. My parents do not living in Canada.
6a. I no go to bed at 10:00.
7a. My wife does not work on Saturdays.

1b. I do not have a job.
2b. They not work at Bo's Restaurant.
3b. We do not like Chinese food.
4b. I do not work on the weekends.
5b. My parents do not live in Canada.
6b. I do not go to bed at 10:00.
7b. My wife no work on Saturdays.

More Negative Statements with Present Tense Verbs

You now know how to make negative sentences that start with **I**, **you**, **we** and **they**. But what about sentences that talk about your sister or your friend or your boss? Study this example:

Misha likes milk. She does not like water.
(A Misha le gusta la leche. No le gusta el agua.)

Notice the following:

▶ The first sentence is affirmative. The second sentence is negative.

▶ In the affirmative sentence, the verb is **likes**, the "s" form of **like**.

▶ In the negative sentence, the first verb or auxiliary verb, is **does**, the "s" form of **do**. The main verb is **like**. Notice that you don't change **like** to **likes**. That's why this sentence is not correct:

~~She does not **likes** milk.~~

Grammar Recipe: To make a negative statement in the present tense when the subject is **he**, **she** or **it**, or one male, female or object (and is not **I** or **you**) place **does not** immediately before the base form of the simple present tense verb.

Here's the pattern:

Subject	does not	Simple present verb	Rest of sentence	Spanish translation
Carolina	does not	speak	English.	Carolina no habla español.

Study these examples of affirmative sentences and negative sentences that include **do not** and **does not**.

Affirmative sentences	Negative sentences
I <u>live</u> in Peru. (Vivo en Perú.)	I <u>do not live</u> in Peru. (No vivo en Perú.)
You <u>live</u> in Peru. (Vives en Perú. Usted vive en Perú.)	You <u>do not live</u> in Peru. (No vives en Perú. Usted no vive en Perú.)
The student <u>lives</u> in Peru. (El estudiante vive en Perú.)	The student <u>does not live</u> in Peru. (El estudiante no vive en Perú.)
Ana <u>lives</u> in Peru. (Ana vive en Perú.)	Ana <u>does not live</u> in Peru. (Ana no vive en Perú.)

5.2.a Directions Rewrite the sentence using a correct verb.

1. Alba (do not, does not) live in Seattle.   Alba does not live in Seattle.
2. Peter (do not, does not) live in Washington D.C.   ....
3. My teacher (do not, does not) live in Florida.   ....
4. I (do not, does not) live in Canada.   ....
5. We (do not, does not) live in Boston.   ....
6. Susan (do not, does not) speak Spanish.   ....
7. Ana (do not, does not) get up early.   ....
8. Juan (do not, does not) like Jennifer Lopez.   ....
9. We (do not, does not) work in Seattle.   ....
10. The teachers (do not, does not) drive to work.   ....

5.2.b Directions: Make each sentence negative. Use **do not** or **does not**.

1. Louisa lives in Chicago.   Louisa does not live in Chicago.
2. Mario lives in New York.   ....
3. Angela lives in Salem.   ....
4. Bruce and Elizabeth live in Paris. ....
5. We live in Seattle.   ....
6. My brother lives in Mexico.   ....
7. I study English at the university. ....
8. Armando studies French.   ....
9. Lucy studies English.   ....
10. I play soccer at the park.   ....

5.2.c Directions: One of the sentences in each pair is not a correct sentence. Cross out the **incorrect** sentence.

1a. She does not live in Havana.   1b. ~~She do not live in Havana.~~
2a. Louisa no living in Canada.   2b. Louisa does not live in Canada.
3a. My sister does not lives in Honduras.   3b. My sister does not live in Honduras.
4a. Patricia does not study English.   4b. Patricia does no study English.
5a. My mother not does work at the hospital. 5b. My mother does not work at the hospital.
6a. Raymundo does not like his apartment.   6b. Raymundo no like his apartment.
7a. Alana does not wash her clothes at the   7b. Alana no is wash her clothes at the
    laundromat (*lavandería)*.   laundromat.
8a. Laura no feel sick today.   8b. Laura does not feel sick today.

5.3 Negative Statements with *Has, Goes* and *Does*

In this section you'll learn about negative statements that include the three present tense irregular verbs you learned about earlier: **have**, **go** and **does.** Consider this conversation and notice the following:

Antonio <u>has</u> a problem. He **doesn't have** a girlfriend.
(Antonio tiene un problema. No tiene novia.)

► The first sentence is affirmative and the second sentence is negative.

► In the affirmative sentence, the verb is **has**, the "**s**" form of **have.**

► In the negative sentence, the first verb or auxiliary verb, is **does**, the "**s**" form of **do.** The main verb is **have.** Notice that you don't change **have** to **has.** That's why this sentence is not correct: ~~She does not has a son.~~

Now read this sentence:

► Angela <u>does not go</u> to school on Saturdays. (Angela no va a la escuela los sábados.)

Notice the following:

► The auxiliary verb changes from **do** to **does** but the main verb, **go**, doesn't change. Thus, it is incorrect to say

~~Angela does not goes to school on Saturdays.~~

► The verb **go** is often followed by the preposition **to** (a).

Here is one final example. Read this sentence:

► Luis <u>does not do</u> his homework. (Luis no hace su tarea.)

In this sentence, the base form of both the auxiliary verb and the main verb is **do.** Here again, you change the auxiliary verb from **do** to **does**, but the main verb, **do**, doesn't change. How confusing is that!

Study these sentences.

Correct sentences	Incorrect sentences
Laura <u>does not have</u> a boyfriend. (Laura no tiene novio.)	**Laura ~~does not has~~ a boyfriend.**
My sister <u>does not go</u> to church on Sundays. (Mi hermana no va a la iglesia los domingos.)	**Mi sister ~~does not goes~~ to church on Sundays.**
Ana sometimes <u>does not do</u> her homework. (Ana a veces no hace su tarea.)	**~~Ana~~ sometimes ~~does not does~~ her homework.**

5.3.a Directions: Underline the correct words so that the sentence is correct.

1. Ana (<u>does not have,</u> does not has) children.

2. Peter (does not goes, does not go) to San Francisco once a year.

3. My teachers (do not have, does not has) new computers.

4. Louis usually (does not do, do not do) homework.

5. The women (do not speak, does not speaks) Spanish.

6. I (do not have, does not have) a large family.

7. My sister and I (do not go, does not go) to church every week.

8. Juana (do not feel, does not feel) sick today.

9. Mr. Lopez (do not have, does not have) a house in Seattle.

5.3.b Directions: Check the sentence in each line that is true for you.

1a.____ My kitchen has a microwave.	1b.____ My kitchen does not have a microwave.
2a.____ My best friend (mejor amigo/a) lives in the United States.	2b.____ My best friend does not live in the United States.
3a.____ I like to swim (*nadar*).	3b.____ I do not like to swim.
4a.____ My bathroom has a shower.	4b.____ My bathroom does not have a shower.
5a.____ I watch television every day.	5b.____ I do not watch television every day.
6a.____ I go to church on Sundays.	6b.____ I do not go to church on Sundays.

5.3.c. Directions: Rewrite this paragraph so that every sentence is negative.

Andrew has a good life. He has a good job. He works. He goes to the mall. He goes to the park to play soccer. He goes dancing. He has a good family. He has nice friends.

Andrew does not have a good life. He does not have a good job.

_____

_____

_____

5.3.d. Directions: Translate these sentences.

1. No tengo perro.   I do not have a dog.

2. Elena no tiene gato.

3. No tenemos una casa grande.

4. Los estudiantes no tienen una buena maestra.

5. No voy a San Francisco los sábados.

6. No hago mi tarea (*homework*).

While using **do not** and **does not** is grammatically correct, it's much more common to use the contractions **don't** and **doesn't**.

▶ **Don't** is a contraction that's made by joining **do** and **not**

▶ **Doesn't** is a contraction made by joining **does** and **not**.

You'll rarely hear someone say

▶ I do not have a job. (No tengo trabajo.)

It's much more common to hear people say

▶ I don't have a job. (No tengo trabajo.)

Similarly, people rarely say

▶ Anita does not have a job. (Anita no tiene trabajo.)

Instead they say

▶ Anita doesn't have a job. (Anita no tiene trabajo.)

Here are several examples of negative statements with and without contractions.

Negative sentences without contractions	Negative sentences with contractions
I <u>do not</u> have a brother. (No tengo un hermano.)	I <u>don't</u> have a brother. (No tengo un hermano.)
You <u>do not</u> study French. (No estudias francés.)	You <u>don't</u> study French. (No estudias francés.)
The nurses <u>do not</u> live in an apartment. (Las enfermeras no viven en un apartamento.)	The nurses <u>don't</u> live in an apartment. (Las enfermeras no viven en un apartamento.)
Umberto <u>does not</u> like grapes. (A Umberto no le gustan las uvas.)	Umberto <u>doesn't</u> like grapes. (A Umberto no le gustan las uvas.)
Ana <u>does not</u> go to work on Saturdays. (Ana no va al trabajo los sábados.)	Ana <u>doesn't</u> go to work on Saturdays. (Ana no va al trabajo los sábados.)
My dress <u>does not</u> need a new button. (Mi vestido no necesita un botón nuevo.)	My dress <u>doesn't</u> need a new button. (Mi vestido no necesita un botón nuevo.)

5.4.a Directions: Make each sentence negative. In the first sentence don't use a contraction. In the second sentence, use a contraction.

1. Martha works five days a week.

    1a.   Martha does not work five days a week.

    1b.   Martha doesn't work five days a week.

2. My sister lives in Panama.

    2a.

    2b.

3. Gabriela and Andrew eat dinner at home on Saturdays.

    3a.

    3b.

4. Julio speaks Italian.

    4a.

    4b.

5. I like cheese.

    5a.

    5b.

6. I have a small kitchen.

    6a.

    6b.

5.4.b Directions: Read the paragraph. Write **T** if the statement is *True* and **F** if the statement is *False*.

Our apartment is very small. It doesn't have a bedroom. We sleep on the couch in the living room. The apartment has a very small bathroom. It has a shower but it doesn't have a bathtub (*tina*). It has a very small kitchen. The kitchen doesn't have a table. We eat on the couch in the living room. The apartment is very dark (*oscuro*). We want to move (*mudarnos*), but the rents (*aquiláres*) are very expensive. Before we move, we need better jobs (*mejores trabajos*).

1. The apartment is very big.   F

2. The apartment has a bedroom.

3. The living room has a couch.

4. They sleep in the bedroom.

5. Their bathroom has a shower.

6. They eat in the kitchen.

7. They want to move.

8. Rents are cheap.

One of the most confusing parts of English grammar is knowing when to use **isn't** and when to use **doesn't**. Consider this example:

Do you know why you use **isn't** in the first sentence and **doesn't** in the second? It all depends on the verb. Consider this affirmative sentence:

▶   Antonio is happy.

The verb is **is**, a form of the verb **to be**.

To make this sentence negative, you'd say,

> ▶ Antonio is not happy. / Antonio isn't happy.*

Now consider this affirmative sentence.

> ▶ He has a girlfriend.

The verb is **has**. Since **has** is <u>not</u> a form of the verb **to be**, you use **does not** or **doesn't** to make this sentence negative. So, you'd say

> ▶ He does not have a girlfriend / He doesn't have a girlfriend.

Grammar recipe:

> ▶ When an affirmative statement includes a form of the verb **to be** (**ser** or **estar**), make the sentence negative by placing **not** after that verb. Or replace the verb with the appropriate negative contraction of the verb **to be**.
>
> > I am tired. -------> I am not tired. / I'm not tired.

> ▶ When an affirmative statement includes a present tense verb that <u>isn't</u> a form of the verb **to be**, you usually make the sentence negative by placing **do not**, **don't**, **does not** or **doesn't** before the verb.
>
> > I work. -------> I do not work. / I don't work.

Study this chart.*

Affirmative statement	Is the verb a form of **to be**?	Negative statement
Lucas <u>is</u> a doctor. (Lucas es médico.)	Yes it is, so use a form of the verb **to be** in the negative statement.	**Lucas <u>is not</u> a doctor. Lucas <u>isn't</u> a doctor.** (Lucas no es médico.)
Lucas <u>has</u> a doctor. (Lucas tiene médico.)	No it isn't, so use **does not** or **doesn't** in the negative statement.	**Lucas <u>does not</u> have a doctor. Lucas <u>doesn't</u> have a doctor.** (Lucas no tiene médico.)

*If you want to review contractions with the verb to be, see Appendix B.

5.5.a Directions: Underline the correct answer.

1. She _____ my mother.   a. <u>isn't</u> b. doesn't

2. I _____ eat lunch at 2:00.   a. am not b. don't

3. He _____ at school.   a. isn't   b. doesn't

4. Eva _____ get up at 8:30.   a. isn't b. doesn't

5. I _____ speak French.   a. am not b. don't

6. We _____ study every day.   a. aren't b. don't

7. The men _____ hungry.   a. aren't b. don't

8. Ana _____ live in Oregon.   a. isn't b. doesn't

9. They _____ in Texas.   a. aren't b. don't

10. I _____ have a break.   a. am not b. don't

5.5.b Directions: Make each sentence negative. Use contractions when you can.

1. I live in Hawaii.   I don't live in Hawaii.

2. We have a dog.

3. I am tired.

4. She works at a restaurant.

5. Juana needs a car.

6. Her garden is beautiful.

7. The cooks are tired.

8. We study English every day.

9. My son has a good teacher.

10. Andrea is my cousin.

5.5.c Directions: Change this paragraph so it is negative. Use contractions where you can.

I'm happy. I like my job. My job is interesting. I have enough (*suficiente*) money. I'm in love with my husband. I live in a nice house. I have a yard. I like my life.

I'm not happy. I don't like my job.

5.5.d Directions: One of the sentences in each line is not correct. Cross out the incorrect sentence.

1a. ~~I no living in Texas.~~
2a. Louisa isn't a doctor.
3a. My brother doesn't have a job.
4a. Patricia isn't a student.
5a. My father no is work at that restaurant.
6a. We no like Chinese food.
7a. The laundromat isn't closed (*cerrada*).
8a. We don't aren't married.

1b. I don't live in Texas.
2b. Louisa doesn't a doctor.
3b. My brother isn't has a job.
4b. Patricia no is student.
5b. My father doesn't work at that restaurant.
6b. We don't like Chinese food.
7b. The laundromat doesn't is closed.
8b. We aren't married.

5.6   Asking *Yes/No* Questions with *Do* and *Does*

In this section, you'll learn to ask yes/no questions with **do** and **does**. Remember that a *yes/no* question is a question whose answer is usually either **yes** or **no**. Here's the pattern:

Verb do or does	Subject	Main verb	Rest of sentence	Spanish translation
Do	you	have	a job?	¿Tienes trabajo?
Does	Anita	have	a job?	¿Tiene trabajo Anita?

Notice the following:

▶ You start the yes/no question with **Does** when the subject of the sentence is **he**, **she**, **it**, or one male, female or thing that is not **I** or **you**.

▶ You start the question with **Do** all other times.

Here are more examples of yes/no questions that start with **do** or **does**.

▶ Do you play soccer twice a week? (¿Juegas al fútbol dos veces por semana?)

▶ Do your parents need a car? (¿Necesitan un carro tus padres?)

▶ Does your sister have a job? (¿Tiene trabajo tu hermana?)

▶ Does Mario work five days a week? (¿Trabaja cinco días por semana Mario?)

You'll learn how to answer these questions in the next section.

Grammar Review: Other kinds of *yes/no* questions

As you now know, not all *yes/no* questions start with **Do** or **Does**. Here are some examples of *yes/no* questions that start with a form of the verb **to be**:

▶ Are you tired? (¿Estás cansado? ¿Estás cansada?)

▶ Is your brother in Mexico? (¿Está en México tu hermano?)

▶ Are your friends from China? (¿Son de China tus amigos?)

And here are some examples of *yes/no* questions that start with **Is there** or **Are there**:

▶ Is there a pencil in your backpack? (¿Hay un lápiz en tu mochila?)

▶ Are there students from Russia in your class? (¿Hay estudiantes de Rusia en tu clase?)

If you want to review questions that start with the verb **to be**, see *Gramática del inglés: Paso a paso 1*. To review **Is there/Are there** questions, go to Chapter 3 of this book.

5.6.a Directions: Write **Q** if the sentence is a **question** and **S** if the sentence is a **statement**. Then put a period or a question mark in the space provided.

	Is this a statement or a question?	Punctuation
1. Do you like pizza	1a. Q	1b. ?
2. Do you have a job	2a.	2b.
3. Juan doesn't work at night	3a.	3b.
4. We don't have books in Spanish	4a.	4b.
5. She doesn't live in an apartment	5a.	5b.
6. Does Amelia work here	6a.	6b.
7. Do you need a ticket (boleto)	7a.	7b.
8. Does your husband speak English	8a.	8b.

5.6.b Directions: Arrange the words so that they make a question. Don't forget to end each question with a question mark (**?**).

1. you / work / Do _____ Do _____ you _____ work? _____
2. you / speak / Do / English _____ _____ _____
3. like / Do / apples / you _____ _____ _____
4. Do / in / you / live / Canada _____ _____ _____
5. car / you / need / Do / a _____ _____ _____
6. soccer / you / Do / play _____ _____
7. Ana / Spanish / speak / Does _____ _____
8. Does / here / Jose / live _____ _____

5.6.c Directions: Read the story. Then, complete the questions using **do** or **does**. Then answer using one of the answers in the box.

Yes, she does.   Yes, he does.   Yes, they do.

11. No, she doesn't.   No, he doesn't.   No, they don't.

It is Saturday afternoon. Patricia Romanoff and Alexander Mendoza feel lonely (*solitarios/solos*). They are married but don't have children. They don't have many friends. They are poor (*pobres*). Patricia wants to buy a sofa, but she doesn't have money. Alexander wants to buy a car, but he doesn't have money. They go to a movie (*película*). They like the movie. It is very funny (*chistosa*). Then, they feel much better.

1a. _Do_ Patricia and Alexander have children?   1b. _No, they don't._

2a. _____ Patricia and Alexander have many friends?   2b _____

3a. _____ Patricia and Alexander have a lot of money?   3b. _____

4a. _____ Patricia want to buy a sofa?   4b. _____

5a. _____ Alexander want to buy a car?   5b. _____

6a. _____ they go to a movie?   6b. _____

7a. _____ they feel better after the movie?   7b _____

5.7 Answering *Yes/No Questions* with *Do* and *Does*

Now that you know how to ask yes/no questions, you're ready to answer them. Study this conversation between two friends waiting for the bus. Notice the following:

► There aren't complete Spanish translations for responses to these *yes/no* questions. That's because, in Spanish, you usually answer such questions with a simple sí or no.

► Because **don't** is a contraction for **do not,** you also could answer the first question,

No, I do not.

► You can also give long answers to these questions. For example, you could answer the first question,

No, I don't have a car. / No, I do not have a car.

Long answers are correct but less common than short answers.

Grammar Recipe: Answering *Yes/No questions* that include **do** or **does**:

► If the question begins with **do**, include **do**, **do not** or **don't** in the answer.

► If the question begins with **does**, include **does**, **does not** or **doesn't** in the answer.

The following chart summarizes how to answer *yes/no* questions that start with **Do** or **Does**.

Yes/No questions and answers with **do** and **does**	
<u>**Do**</u> **you work today?** (¿Trabajas hoy?) 　**Yes, I** <u>do</u>. (Sí.) 　**No, I** <u>don't</u>. (No.) 　**No, I** <u>do not.</u> (No.)	<u>**Does**</u> **Jose work today?** (¿Trabaja José hoy?) <u>**Does**</u> **he work today?** (¿Trabaja él hoy? 　**Yes, he** <u>does</u>. (Sí.) 　**No, he** <u>doesn't</u>. (No.) 　**No, he** <u>does not</u>. (No.)
<u>**Do**</u> **Mario and Jose work today?** (¿Trabajan Mario y José hoy?) <u>**Do**</u> **they work today?** (¿Trabajan ellos hoy?) 　**Yes, they** <u>do</u>. (Sí.) 　**No, they** <u>don't</u>. (No.) 　**No, they** <u>do not</u>. (No.)	<u>**Does**</u> **Anita work today?** (¿Trabaja Anita hoy?) <u>**Does**</u> **she work today?** (¿Trabaja ella hoy?) 　**Yes, she** <u>does</u>. (Sí.) 　**No she** <u>doesn't</u>. (No.) 　**No, she** <u>does not</u>. (No.)

5.7.a Directions: Underline the correct answer.

1. Does your mother live in the U.S?
   a. <u>Yes, she does.</u>   b. Yes, I do.

2. Do you live in California?
   a. Yes, she does.   b. Yes, I do.

3. Does Carlos get up early?
   a. Yes, he does.   b. Yes, I do.

4. Do the students go to school on Saturday?
   a. No, he doesn't.   b. No, they don't.

5. Does Anita play soccer?
   a. No, she doesn't.   b. No, I don't.

6. Does your aunt live here?
   a. No, she doesn't.   b. No, they don't.

7. Does your boss speak Spanish?
   a. Yes, I do.   b. Yes, she does.

8. Do you speak Italian?
   a. No, I don't.   b. No, she doesn't.

5.7.b Directions: Answer each question affirmatively. First give a short answer. Then give a long answer.

1. Do you like pizza?

   1a. Yes, I do.

   1b. Yes, I like pizza.

2. Do you work at a restaurant?

   2a. _____

   2b. _____

3. Does your sister live in the U.S.?

   3a. _____

   3b. _____

4. Do your parents speak English?

   4a. _____

   4b. _____

5.7.c Directions: Answer each question negatively. First give a short answer. Then give a long answer.

1. Do you have a job?

   1a. No, I don't.

   1b. No, I don't have a job.

2. Do you like American food (*comida*)?

   2a. _____

   2b. _____

3. Does your brother live in Mexico?

   3a. _____

   3b. _____

4. Does your kitchen have a microwave?

   4a. _____

   4b. _____

You've already learned some tips for knowing when to use **isn't** and when to use **doesn't** in negative sentences. These same rules apply to answering *yes/no* questions. Consider this example.

Do you know why the response is **Yes, I am** to the first question and **Yes, I do** to the second? Here again, it all depends on the verb.

Grammar recipe

▶ When a *yes/no* question includes a form of the verb **to be** (ser or estar) respond with a short answer that includes a form of the verb **to be**. (**Yes, I am; No, I'm not; Yes, she is**; etc.)

▶ When a *yes/no* question includes **do** or **does**, respond with a short answer that includes **do** or **does**. (**Yes, I do; No, I don't**; etc.)

Study this table:

Preguntas cerradas con do y does	Preguntas cerradas con to be

<u>Do</u> you have a house in Mexico? (¿Tienes una casa en México?)
   Yes, I <u>do</u>. (Sí.)
   No, I <u>do</u> <u>not</u>. (No.)
   No, I <u>don't</u>. (No.)
	Are you from Mexico? (¿Eres de México?)
	   Yes, I <u>am</u>. (Sí.)
	   No, I <u>am not</u>. (No.)
	   No, I'<u>m</u> <u>not</u>. (No.)

Do your parents live in Mexico? (¿Viven en México tus padres?)
   Yes, they <u>do</u>. (Sí.)
   No, they <u>do not</u>. (No.)
   No, they <u>don't</u>. (No.)
	Are your parents in Mexico? (¿Están en México tus padres?)
	   Yes, they <u>are</u>. (Sí.)
	   No, they <u>are not</u>. (No.)
	   No, they <u>aren't</u>. (No.)
	   No, they'<u>re</u> <u>not</u>. (No.)

Does your sister work in a hospital? (¿Trabaja en un hospital tu hermana?)
   Yes, she <u>does</u>. (Sí.)
   No, she <u>doesn't</u>. (No.)
   No, she <u>does not</u>. (No.)
	Is your sister a doctor? (¿Es médica tu hermana?
	   Yes, she <u>is</u>. (Sí.)
	   No, she <u>is not</u>. (No.)
	   No, she <u>isn't</u>. (No.)
	   No, she'<u>s</u> <u>not</u>. (No.)

5.8.a Directions: Answer these questions about yourself. Answer with

Yes, I am.

No, I'm not.

Yes, I do.

No, I don't.

1. Are you married?

2. Are you in love?

3. Do you have a job?

4. Do you like to study English?

5. Do you live in California?

6. Are you at home now?

7. Do you speak Spanish at home?

8. Are you tired right now (*ahora mismo*)?

9. Do you eat breakfast every day?

10. Do you like scary movies? (*películas de miedo*)

11. Are you a good cook?

5.8.b Directions: Read the story. Then answer the questions with

Yes, he is.

No, he isn't.

Yes, he does.

No, he doesn't.

My name is Diego. I am 27 years old. I live in San Francisco. I live in a beautiful house with my wife and two children. I have a dog and two cats. I am a carpenter (*carpintero*). I make furniture (*muebles*). I go to San Francisco Community College two nights a week. I study English. I am from Honduras. My classmates are from many countries.

1. Is Diego 37 years old?   No, he isn't.

2. Does Diego live in San Francisco?

3. Does Diego live in an apartment?

4. Is Diego married?

5. Does Diego have children?

6. Does Diego have pets (*mascotas*)?

7. Is Diego a teacher?

8. Does Diego make furniture?

9. Is Diego a student?

10. Does Diego study English?

11. Does Diego study mathematics?

12. Is Diego from Honduras?

5.9   *Where, When,* and *What Time* **Questions**

Read this conversation to learn about asking and answering questions that start with question words.

The following table shows you the pattern you use to ask questions in the simple present tense that start with question words **where** (dónde), **when** (cuándo) and **what time** (a qué hora). It also includes possible answers to those questions.

Question word	do or does	Subject	Base verb	Rest of sentence	Answers
Where	do	you	play	soccer?	I play soccer at Hoover Park.
Where	does	Adam	play	soccer?	He plays soccer at Baily Park.
When	do	you	play	soccer?	I play soccer on Tuesdays and Thursdays.
When	does	Adam	play	soccer?	He plays soccer on Sundays.
What time	do	you	play	soccer?	I play soccer at 5:30.
What time	does	Adam	play	soccer?	He plays soccer at 11:00.

Note the following:

▶ The subject of the sentence determines whether to use **do** or **does**. If the subject is **he**, **she**, **it**, or one male, female or thing, use **does**. Otherwise, use **do**.

▶ Many people learning English think the answer to a question that includes **do** or **does** must also include **do** or **does**. For example,

         I do play soccer on Sundays.

         He does play soccer at 5:30.

Although including **do** or **does** is not incorrect, it is only necessary for emphasis.

5.9.a Directions: Arrange the words so that they make a question.

1. you / study / do / Where / English   <u>Where</u>   <u>do</u>   <u>you</u>   <u>study</u>   <u>English?</u>
2. you / study / do / When / English _____
3. your / do / call / you / family / When _____
4. do / eat / What time / they / dinner _____
5. Luis / Where / does / work _____
6. live / Where / does / Julia _____

5.9.b Directions: Underline the correct answer.

1. When does your mother work?

a. <u>She works from Monday to Friday.</u>

b. She works at a restaurant.

2. When do you play soccer?

a. I play soccer in Hooper Park.

b. I play soccer on Tuesdays.

3. What time do you study English?

a. I study English at Brett Adult School.

b. I study English from 8 to 10 p.m.

4. Where do you buy food?

a. I buy food at Andres Market.

b. I buy food on Saturdays.

5. Where does Brenda eat lunch?

a. She eats lunch at Max's Cafe.

b. She eats lunch at noon.

6. What time does your class start?

a. It starts at 9:00.

b. It starts in the afternoon.

7. Where does your sister study English?

a. She studies at San Juan Adult School.

b. She studies Monday to Friday.

8. When do you wash your car?

a. I wash my car on Saturdays.

b. I wash my car at Dedees Car Wash.

5.9.c Directions: Read the story. Then answer the questions. Use complete sentences.

Luis is retired (*jubilado*). He gets up at 9:00. He takes a shower. Then, he goes to Charley's Restaurant. He eats breakfast. He always has three eggs. He drinks a cup of coffee. He reads the newspaper and relaxes. In the afternoon, he goes to the park. He talks to his friends. He walks in the park. At 6:00, he goes home and makes dinner. In the evening, he watches TV in his apartment. He goes to sleep at 11:00. The next day, he does the same thing (*lo mismo*).

1. What time does Luis get up?   <u>He gets up at 9:00.</u>

2. Does he eat breakfast at home? _____

3. Where does he eat breakfast? _____

4. What does he drink? _____

5. When does he go to the park? _____

6. Where does he walk? _____

7. Does he go home at 6:00? _____

8. What time does he go to sleep? _____

Negative statements with **do** and **does**

To make a negative statement in the present tense when the subject is **I**, **we**, **you** or **they**

▶ Place **do not** or **don't** immediately before the base form of the verb.

To make a negative statement in the present tense when the subject is **he**, **she** or **it**, or one male, female or object (and is not **I** or **you**)

▶ Place **does not** or **doesn't** immediately before the base form of the simple present tense verb.

Asking and answering *yes/no* questions with **do** and **does**

You start the yes/no question with **Does** when the subject of the sentence is **he**, **she**, **it**, or one male, female or thing that is not **I** or **you**. You start the question with **Do** all other times.

▶ If the question begins with **do**, include **do**, **do not** or **don't** in the answer.

▶ If the question begins with **does**, include **does**, **does not** or **doesn't** in the answer.

Yes/No questions and answers with **do** and **does***	

<u>Do</u> you work today? (¿Trabajas hoy?)
  Yes, I <u>do</u>. (Sí.)
  No, I <u>don't</u>. (No.)
  No, I <u>do not</u>. (No.)
	<u>Does</u> Jose work today? (¿Trabaja José hoy?)
	<u>Does</u> he work today? (¿Trabaja él hoy?
	  Yes, he <u>does</u>. (Sí.)
	  No, he <u>doesn't</u>. (No.)
	  No, he <u>does not</u>. (No.)

<u>Do</u> Mario and Jose work today? (¿Trabajan Mario y José hoy?)
<u>Do</u> they work today? (¿Trabajan ellos hoy?)
  Yes, they <u>do</u>. (Sí.)
  No, they <u>don't</u>. (No.)
  No, they <u>do not</u>. (No.)
	<u>Does</u> Anita work today? (¿Trabaja Anita hoy?)
	<u>Does</u> she work today? (¿Trabaja ella hoy?)
	  Yes, she <u>does</u>. (Sí.)
	  No she <u>doesn't</u>. (No.)
	  No, she <u>does not</u>. (No.)

Where, *when* and *what time* questions and answers

Question word	do or does	Subject	Base verb	Rest of sentence	Answers
Where	do	you	play	soccer?	I play soccer at Hoover Park.
Where	does	Adam	play	soccer?	He plays soccer at Baily Park.
When	do	you	play	soccer?	I play soccer on Tuesdays and Thursdays.
When	does	Adam	play	soccer?	He plays soccer on Sundays.
What time	do	you	play	soccer?	I play soccer at 5:30.
What time	does	Adam	play	soccer?	He plays soccer at 11:00.

*To review contractions with **to be** see Appendix B.

English Grammar: Step by Step 2

 **More Practice!**

P5.a Directions: Make each sentence negative. Use contractions when you can.

1. Lisa drives to work.   Lisa doesn't drive to work.

2. Mario goes to Atlas Community College.

3. I play soccer on Mondays.

4. The students have homework every day.

5. We live in Seattle.

6. My brother lives in Mexico.

7. I work at a restaurant.

8. My parents like Chinese food.

9. I am tired.

10. I eat lunch at 11:30.

11. They watch television every night.

12. Jose is my uncle.

13. My husband wants a dog.

14. Mary and Justin have two daughters.

15. You are late.

P5.b Directions: Underline the correct words so that the sentence is correct.

1. Myra (doesn't have, doesn't has) a dog.

2. Ana (doesn't go, doesn't goes) to church on Sunday.

3. The student (doesn't have, doesn't has) a pencil.

4. The nurse (doesn't go, doesn't goes) to the hospital.

5. Antonio (doesn't have, doesn't has) a cat.

6. Mauricio (doesn't do, doesn't does) his homework.

7. The kitchen (doesn't have, doesn't has) a blender.

8. The students (don't go, don't goes) to the library.

9. We (do not, does not) study French.

10. My parents (do not, does not) drive to work.

11. We (don't have, doesn't have) a new car.

12. Lisa (isn't, doesn't) know her cousin Mario.a

13. I (am not, do not) at work now.

14. My mother (is not, does not) like meat.

P5.c Directions: Answer the questions using one of the phrases in the box. Tell the truth.

Yes, I do.   Yes, I am.

No, I don't.   No, I'm not.

1. Are you at home now? _____

2. Do you have a job? _____

3. Do you like the United States? _____

4. Are you tired today? _____

5. Are you hungry right now? _____

6. Do you read books in English? _____

7. Are you married? _____

8. Are you in love? _____

9. Do you have a computer? _____

10. Do you need a computer? _____

P5.d Directions: Read the story. Then answer the questions using one of the phrases in the box.

Yes, she does.   Yes, they do.   Yes, she is.   Yes, they are.

No, she doesn't   No, they don't.   No, she isn't.   No, they aren't.

Amanda and Elizabeth are roommates (*compañeras de apartamento*). They live in an apartment. They are cooks. They work at Piñas Mexican Restaurant. But sometimes they argue (*discuten*). Amanda likes the apartment hot. Elizabeth doesn't like the apartment hot. She likes the apartment cold. Amanda likes to sleep late (*tarde*). Elizabeth doesn't like to sleep late. She gets up early (*temprano*). They both like television. But Amanda likes telenovelas. Elizabeth likes sports (*deportes*). One day Amanda moves (*se muda*) to a new apartment. Now they don't argue. They talk on the telephone everyday. They are good friends.

1. Do Amanda and Elizabeth live in a house?   No, they don't.

2. Is Elizabeth a waitress?   _____

3. Do Amanda and Elizabeth argue?   _____

4. Does Amanda like the apartment cold?   _____

5. Does Elizabeth like the apartment cold?   _____

6. Does Amanda like to sleep late?   _____

7. Does Elizabeth like to sleep late?   _____

8. Does Amanda like telenovelas?   _____

9. Does Elizabeth like television?   _____

10. Does Elizabeth move to a different apartment?   _____

11. Are Amanda and Elizabeth friends now?   _____

12. Do they talk on the phone every day?   _____

P5.e Directions: Arrange the words so that they make a question. Don't forget to end each question with a question mark (?).

1. you / work / do / Where ___Where___ ___do___ ___you___ ___work?___

2. you / work / do / When _____ _____ _____ _____

3. buy / does / shoes / Lucy / Where _____ _____ _____ _____ _____

4. does / play / Where / soccer / Ana _____ _____ _____ _____ _____

5. lunch / you / What time / do / eat _____ _____ _____ _____ _____

6. work / When / does / Jose _____ _____ _____ _____

P5.f Directions: Underline the correct answer.

1. Does your sister live in Honduras?
a. <u>Yes, she does.</u>   b. Yes, I do.

2. Are you at work now?
a. Yes, I am.   b. Yes, I do.

3. Is Silvia a doctor?
a. Yes, she is.   b. Yes, she does.

4. Do the painters work on Saturday?
a. No, he doesn't.   b. No, they don't.

5. Are your parents at home?
a. Yes, they are.   b. Yes, they do.

6. Does Frank play tennis every week?
a. No, I don't.   b. No, he doesn't.

7. Does your boss speak Spanish?
a. No, she doesn't.   b. No, they don't.

8. Does your boss speak English?
a. Yes, she is.   b. Yes, she does.

9. Do you speak Italian?
a. No, I don't.   b. No, she I don't.

10. Does Lucinda need a computer?
a. No, she isn't.   b. No, she doesn't.

P5.g Directions: Translate these sentences. Use contractions when you can.

1. No tengo carro. _____ I don't have a car._____

2. Mi hija no es enfermera. Es doctor. _____

3. Mi madre no vive en Houston. Vive en Atlanta. _____

4. Tengo dos trabajos (*jobs*). _____

5. Mi hermanas no hablan inglés. _____

6. Mi cocina no es grande. Es pequeña. _____

7. Mi esposo no quiere un perro. _____

8. No estoy feliz porque (*because*) no tengo carro. _____

9. A mi hija no le gusta la pizza. _____

10. Mis amigos no están en el parque. Están en la escuela. _____

P5.h Directions: Translate these questions.

1. ¿Tienes un carro? _____ Do you have a car?_____

2. ¿Hablas inglés? _____

3. ¿Vives en Chicago? _____

4. ¿Te sientes enfermo? _____

5. ¿Trabajas en Pop's Pizza? _____

6. ¿Tu hermana tiene carro? _____

7. ¿Tu hermano habla inglés? _____

8. ¿Liliana vive en Miami? _____

Chapter 6

I'm studying English now.

In the last two chapters you learned how to talk about activities that you do routinely. In this chapter, you'll learn how to talk about what you're doing right now. To do this you'll use the **present progressive** verb tense.

At the end of this chapter you will be able to

- use present progressive verbs in affirmative and negative sentences.
- spell present progressive verbs.
- ask and answer questions about what you're doing right now.
- know when to use simple present verbs and when to use present progressive verbs.

Both English and Spanish have two tenses that are used to speak about activities that occur in the present: *simple present* and *present progressive*.

▶ You use the *simple present tense* to talk about activities you perform regularly and to state facts and express feelings.

▶ You use the *present progressive tense* (also called the **present continuous tense**) to talk about what you're doing right now.

Study this conversation:

What are you doing?
(¿Qué estás haciendo?
¿Qué haces?)

I'm studying English.
(Estoy estudiando inglés.
Estudio inglés.)

Did you noitce that there are two translations for **"What are you doing?"** and **"I 'm studying English."**? In reality, Spanish speakers talking about what they're doing now are just as likely to use the simple present tense as they are to use the present progressive tense. In contrast, English speakers almost always use the present progressive tense to talk about what's happening right now.

A present progressive verb has two parts:

▶ The form of the verb **to be** that matches the subject of the sentence. Note that in this case, the verb **to be** acts as an *auxiliary verb* or *helping verb*.

▶ The *present participle* (the base form of the verb followed by **ing**).

English vs. Spanish: In Spanish, the present participle is equivalent to verbs that end in ando and iendo. For example hablando, comiendo and trabajando.

Sentences in the present progressive tense have this form:

Subject	Verb **to be**	Present participle (Base Verb + **ing**)	Spanish translation
I	am	working.	Yo estoy trabajando. Yo trabajo.

The following table shows how to conjugate present progressive verbs.

I <u>am working</u>.	He <u>is working</u>.	We <u>are working</u>.
	She <u>is working</u>.	You <u>are working</u>.
	It <u>is working</u>.	They <u>are working</u>.

Notice that the **ing** form of the verb, the present participle, never changes, regardless of the form of the verb **to be** that precedes it.

6.1.a Directions: Underline the present participle. Remember that the present participle ends in **ing.**

1. talks	<u>talking</u>	talk
2. work	works	working
3. eats	eat	eating
4. plays	playing	play
5. going	go	goes
6. do	doing	does
7. brushing	brush	brushes
8. cleans	clean	cleaning

6.1.b Directions: Using the present progressive verb tense, complete each sentence using the correct form of the verb **sleep** (*dormir*).

1. I ___am___ sleeping. _____
2. You _____ _____
3. He _____ _____
4. She _____ _____
5. It _____ _____
6. We _____ _____

7. Edgar _____ _____
8. Sam _____ _____
9. The children _____
10. Ed and I _____
11. The men _____
12. That woman _____

6.1.c Directions: Using the present progressive verb tense, complete each sentence using the correct form of the verb **work** (*trabajar*).

1. I ___am___ working. _____
2. You _____ _____
3. He _____ _____
4. She _____ _____
5. It _____ _____
6. We _____ _____

7. Edgar _____ _____
8. The teacher _____ _____
9. That man _____ _____
10. Dan and Jim _____
11. Bob and I _____
12. The women _____

6.1.d Directions: Using the present progressive verb tense, complete each sentence using the correct form of the verb **read** (*leer*).

1. We ___are___ reading. _____
2. You _____ _____
3. Arnold _____ _____
4. She _____ _____

5. I _____ _____
6. The teachers _____ _____
7. That child _____ _____
8. Peter _____ _____

As you now know, present participles are usually formed by adding **ing** to the base form of the verb. There are, however, a few present participles that are spelled a little bit differently. This page explains how to spell these exceptions.

Verbs ending in an **e** preceded by a consonant

Consider the verb **dance** (bailar). The present participle of **dance** is **dancing**, not ~~**danceing**~~. How do you know? Follow this rule:

▸ If a base verb ends in an **e** preceded by a consonant, make the present participle by dropping the **e** and adding **ing**.

▸ The base verb, **dance**, ends in an **e** preceded by the consonant **c**, so you drop the **e**, then add **ing**.

Here are some verbs where you apply this rule:

Vocabulary: Verbs ending in **e** preceded by a consonant		
make/making (hacer/haciendo)	**take/taking** (llevar/llevando, tomar/ tomando)	**dance/dancing** (bailar/bailando)
prepare/preparing (preparar/preparando)	**drive/driving** (manejar/ manejando)	

Verbs ending in a consonant preceded by a vowel

Consider the verb **cut** (cortar). The present participle is **cutting**, not ~~**cuting**~~. How do you know? Follow this rule:

▸ If a base verb is one syllable and ends in a consonant preceded by a vowel, make the past participle by doubling the consonant, then adding **ing**.

The base verb, **cut**, ends in a consonant, **t**, preceded by a vowel **u**, so you double the **t** before adding **ing**. Note that this rule doesn't apply to verbs ending in **x**, **y** or **w**.

Here are some verbs where you apply this rule:

Vocabulary: Verbs ending in a consonant preceded by a vowel	
run/running (correr/ corriendo)	**put/putting** (poner/poniendo)
sit/sitting (sentarse/sentándose)	**cut/cutting** (cortar/cortando)

6.2.a Directions: Complete with the present participle.

base form	present participle	base form	present participle
1. fix	fixing	9. brush	
2. watch		10. write (*escribir*)	
3. study		11. carry	
4. relax		12. put	
5. speak		13. play	
6. pay		14. listen (*escuchar*)	
7. go		15. run	
8. sit		16. drive	

6.2.b Directions: Choose the correct verb from the words below. Then, write the present participle of that verb to complete the sentence. Use each verb once.

brush	drive	take	play
watch	speak	prepare	cut

1. My mother is ___preparing___ dinner.

2. We are _____ to work.

3. My friends are _____ television.

4. Luis is _____ a shower.

5. I am _____ my teeth.

6. I don't understand because they are _____ French.

7. I am _____ the pizza.

8. The girls are _____ baseball in the park.

6.2.c Directions: Translate these sentences.

1. Estoy leyendo un libro.   I am reading a book.

2. Susan está bailando.

3. Irma está mirando televisión.

4. Estamos estudiando inglés.

5. Las niñas están durmiendo.

6. Lilian está trabajando y Lucas está en la escuela.

Making negative sentences that include a present progressive verb is easy: Just use the correct form of the verb **to be** followed by **not**, followed by the present participle or **ing** form of the verb. For example,

▶ **He is not studying.** (Él no está estudiando. Él no estudia.)

Negative sentences in the present progressive tense have this form:

Subject	Verb to be	not	Present participle (Base Verb + ing)	Spanish translation
I	am	not	working.	No estoy trabajando. No trabajo.

Here are some examples of affirmative and negative sentences that include a present progressive verb.

Affirmative sentences	Negative sentences
I am studying.	I am <u>not</u> studying.
We are studying.	We are <u>not</u> studying.
They are studying.	They are <u>not</u> studying.

Common Errors with Present Progressive Verbs

One common error made by people learning to use present progressive verbs is to include the present participle but to omit the verb **to be**. This is the case with the sentences in the right column in the table below.

Correct sentences	Incorrect sentences
I am eating breakfast.	I ~~eating~~ breakfast.
She is watching TV.	She ~~watching~~ TV.
Luis and Henry are not playing soccer.	Luis and Henry ~~not playing~~ soccer. Luis and Henry ~~no playing~~ soccer.

Another common mistake is to forget to add **ing** to the base form of the verb. This is the case with the sentences in the right column in the table below.

Correct sentences	Incorrect sentences
I am eating breakfast.	I ~~am eat~~ breakfast.
She is watching TV.	She ~~is watch~~ TV.
Luis and Henry are not playing soccer.	Luis and Henry ~~are not play~~ soccer. Luis and Henry ~~no play~~ soccer.

6.3.a Directions: Make each affirmative sentence negative. Do not use contractions.

1. I am working. _I am not working._
2. They are watching television. _____
3. She is reading. _____
4. We are driving home from work. _____
5. It is raining (lloviendo). _____
6. They are running in the park. _____
7. He is preparing lunch. _____
8. I am talking to my sister. _____
9. We are walking to the mall. _____

6.3.b Directions: Each of the following sentences contains an error that is underlined. Rewrite the sentence so that it includes a correct present progressive verb.

1. I <u>am study</u> Spanish. _I am studying Spanish._
2. The students <u>are play</u> soccer. _____
3. We <u>are no working</u> now. _____
4. The children <u>playing</u> at the park. _____
5. They <u>are read</u> now. _____
6. Laura <u>she sitting</u> in the kitchen. _____
7. Antonio <u>is sleep</u> now. _____
8. My parents <u>not visit</u> my sister. _____
9. I am <u>no sleeping</u>. _____
10. They <u>no talking</u>. _____

6.3.c Directions: Translate these sentences. Do not use contractions.

1. No estoy trabajando ahora. _I am not working now._
2. No estoy estudiando ahora. _____
3. Marlene no está durmiendo. _____
4. Los niños no están jugando ahora. _____
5. Mi padre no está comiendo. _____

6.4 Contractions

As you know, a *contraction* is a word that is made by combining two other words. You'll often use both affirmative and negative contractions with the verb **to be** when you are using the present progressive tense. Study this conversation and note the following:

What is Carlos doing? (¿Qué está haciendo Carlos? ¿Qué hace Carlos?)

He's playing video games. He isn't doing his homework. (Está jugando a los videojuegos./Juega a los videojuegos. No está haciendo la tarea./No hace la tarea.)

▶ The contraction **he's** is a short form of **he is**.

▶ The contraction **isn't** is a short form of **is not**.

Using contractions with present progressive verbs is easy: Simply use the appropriate contraction with the verb **to be**, either affirmative or negative, followed by the present participle.

Affirmative sentences with contractions in the present progressive tense have this form:

Contraction with pronoun and the verb to be	Present participle	Spanish translation
He's	working.	Él está trabajando. Él trabaja.

Negative sentences with contractions in the present progressive tense have this form:

Subject and negative contraction*	Present participle	Spanish translation
He isn't	working.	Él no está trabajando. Él no trabaja.
He's not	working.	

Study this list for more examples of affirmative and negative sentences with contraction that use the present progressive tense.

▶ **I'm working.** (Yo estoy trabajando. Yo trabajo.)

▶ **I'm not working.** (Yo no estoy trabajando. Yo no trabajo.)

▶ **They're reading.** (Ellos están leyendo. Ellos leen.)

▶ **They're not reading. They aren't reading.** (Ellos no están leyendo. Ellos no leen.)

▶ **He's playing soccer.** (Él está jugando al fútbol. Él juega al fútbol.)

6. **He's not playing soccer. He isn't playing soccer.** (Él no está jugando al fútbol. Él no juega al fútbol.)

*To review affirmative and negative contractions with the verb **to be**, see Appendix B.

6.4.a Directions: Rewrite each of these affirmative sentences so that it includes a contraction.

1. I am reading.   I'm reading.

2. They are playing soccer.

3. She is working.

4. We are walking to work.

5. It is raining (*lloviendo*).

6. They are carrying their books.

7. He is repairing his car.

8. I am taking a shower.

6.4.b Directions: Rewrite each of these negative sentences so that it includes a contraction.

1. She is not working today.   She isn't working today.

2. They are not brushing their teeth.

3. She is not taking a shower.

4. We are not visiting your parents.

5. It is not raining.

6. He is not sitting in his car.

7. He is not talking to his girlfriend.

8. I am not playing the violin.

6.4.c Directions: Each of the following sentences contains an error that is underlined. Rewrite the sentence so that it includes a contraction and a correct present progressive verb.

1. I <u>am study</u> French.   I'm studying French.

2. They <u>are work</u> at an airport (*aeropuerto*).

3. We <u>no work</u> six days a week.

4. He <u>no is walk</u> to school.

5. They <u>no listen</u> to music.

6. We <u>reading</u> in the kitchen.

7. She <u>no is sleep</u> now.

8. I <u>am visit</u> my daughter in Colorado.

6.5　*Yes/No* Questions and Answers

To learn about *yes/no* questions with present progressive verbs, read this conversation between mother and daughter talking on their cell phones.

Are you walking to school now?
(¿Estás caminando a la escuela ahora?)

Yes, I am.
(Sí.)

Are you using your umbrella?
(¿Estás usando tu paraguas?)

No, I'm not.
(No.)

Grammar recipe: To create a *yes/no* question in the present progressive tense:

► Start with the appropriate form of the verb **to be**.

► Add the subject (a noun or pronoun).

► Add the present participle.

Yes/no questions that include a present progressive verb have this form:

Verb **to be**	Noun or pronoun	Present participle	Spanish translation
Are	**you**	**studying?**	¿Estás estudiando? ¿Estudias?

You answer these questions the same way you answer other *yes/no* questions with the verb t**o be**. Study this table.

Yes/No questions **with present progressive verbs**

Are you studying?
　Yes, I am.
　No, I am not.
　No, I'm not.

Are Laura and I studying? Are we studying?
　Yes, we are.
　No, we are not.
　No, we're not. No we aren't.

Is Peter studying? Is he studying?
　Yes, he is.
　No, he is not.
　No, he isn't. No, he's not.

Are the boys studying? Are they studying?
　Yes, they are.
　No, they are not.
　No, they're not. No, they aren't.

Is Ana studying? Is she studying?
　Yes, she is.
　No, she is not.
　No, she isn't. No, she's not.

6.5.a Directions: Begin each question with **Is** or **Are**. Then look at the picture and answer each question using one of the responses below.

Yes, he is.   Yes, she is.   Yes, they are.

No, he isn't.   No, she isn't.   No, they aren't.

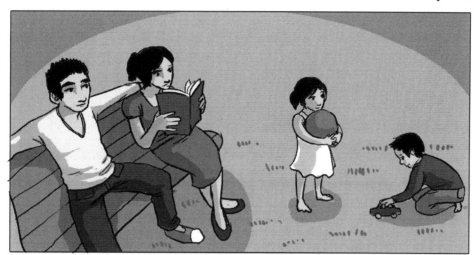

1. __Are_____ the parents playing with their children?   No, they aren't. ____

2. _____ Dad talking to his children? _____

3. _____ Mom sitting (*sentada*) next to Dad? _____

4. _____ Mom reading? _____

5. _____ the parents singing (*cantando*)? _____

6. _____ the children at home? _____

7. _____ the children at the park? _____

8. _____ the boy playing with a car? _____

9. _____ the boy playing with his sister? _____

10. _____ the girl playing with a ball? _____

11. _____ the girl talking to her mother? _____

6.5.b Directions: Arrange the words so that they make a question. Don't forget to end each question with a question mark (**?**).

Are   you   working?

1. you / working / Are _____

2. now / working / Is / Juana _____

3. you / going / home / Are _____

4. Is / studying / Caroline / now _____

5. they /Are / home / at _____

6. dinner / Is / Ernesto / eating _____

7. sleeping / you /Are _____

8. Does / here / Jose / live _____

The most common *question word* questions used with present progressive verbs ask people what they're doing and where they're going.

Question word questions that include a present progressive verb have this form:

Question word	Verb **to be**	Subject	Present participle (Base Verb + **ing**)	Spanish translation
Where	**are**	**you**	**going?**	¿Adónde vas?
What	**is**	**Juan**	**doing?**	¿Qué hace Juan?
When	**are**	**they**	**working?**	¿Cuándo trabajan ellos?

Here are the answers to the questions above.

Subject	Verb **to be**	Present participle	Rest of sentence	Spanish translation
I	**am**	**going**	**to work.**	Estoy yendo al trabajo. Voy al trabajo.
He	**is**	**watching**	**television.**	Él está mirando televisión. Él mira televisión.
They	**are**	**working**	**in the morning.**	Ellos están trabajando por la mañana. Ellos trabajan por la mañana.

Here are more questions, along with their answers.

- ► Where are the students going? They're going to their class.
- ► What are they studying? They are studying mathematics.
- ► Why are they studying? They are studying because (*porque*) they have an exam.

6.6.a Directions: Answer the questions about the students in the classroom. Use present progressive verbs. Use contractions when you can. Use the verbs in the box. Use each verb once.

drink   eat   read   sleep   talk   write

1. What is Ana doing?   She's reading.

2. What is Luke doing?

3. What are Bev and Alex doing?

4. What is Mark doing?

5. What are Lucy and Sue doing?

6. What is Miguel doing?

6.6.b Directions: Each question has one answer. Write the letter of the correct answer on the line.

  E.   1. Are you sleeping?   a. I am watching a movie.

       2. What are you listening to?   b. I am listening to music.

       3. What is Carlos doing?   c. Because I have a test (*una prueba/un examen*).

       4. Why are you studying?   d. She is going to San Francisco.

       5. Where is Emily going?   e. No, I'm not.

       6. What are you watching?   f. He is playing basketball.

       7. What is Carla reading?   g. No, she isn't.

       8. Is your sister playing soccer?   h. She is reading the newspaper. (*el periódico*)

6.6.c Directions: Each of the following questions contains an error. Rewrite the questions so that it includes a correct present progressive verb.

1. What you doing?   What are you doing?

2. Where you going?

3. Why you crying (*llorando*)?

4. What Alberto doing?

5. Where he going?

6.7 Present Progressive Verbs vs. Simple Present Verbs

Knowing when to use simple present verbs and when to use present progressive verbs is one of the most challenging aspects of learning English. Consider this conversation between two brothers.

The first question and answer use the *present progressive tense* because they refer to an activity that is occurring right now. The second question and answer use the *simple present tense* because they refer to a habitual activity.

This table summarizes how these two tenses are used. But this is not a definitive list. There are many subtle differences that you'll learn about as you continue your study of English.

Verb tense	How this verb tense is used	Examples
Present progressive*	To express actions that are occurring right now	Juan is eating lunch now.
Simple present	To express habitual actions	I always eat lunch at 1:00.
	To express facts, feelings and desires**	My mother has three sons. The children like ice cream.

The following table compares the use the present progressive and simple present verb tenses.

	Present progressive	Simple present
Affirmative and negative statements	Lucas is studying now. Lucas is not studying now.	Lucas studies English at home. Lucas doesn't study English at home.
Yes/no questions and answers	Are you working now? Yes, I am. No, I am not.	Do you work on Saturdays? Yes, I do. No, I don't.
Question word questions and answers	What are you doing? I am watching TV. I'm watching TV.	What do you usually do on Saturday afternoons? I play soccer.

*The present progressive tense can also be used to talk about actions that occur in the future, but that's beyond the scope of this book

**You sometimes use verbs that express facts, feelings and desires in the present progressive tense, but that discussion is beyond the scope of this book.

6.7.a Directions: Underline the correct verb. Then write whether the verb is *simple present* or *present progressive*.

1. I (study, <u>am studying</u>) now.   present progressive

2. My uncle (studies, is studying) English every day.

3. I (know, am knowing) your sister.

4. Maria always (works, is working) five days a week.

5. My boyfriend (has, is having) a good job.

6. I (watch, am watching) TV now.

7. I usually (watch, am watching) TV in the afternoon.

8. Quiet! (*¡Cállate!*) We (listen, are listening) to music.

6.7.b Directions: Read the story. Then, answer the questions. Use the answers below.

Yes, he is.   Yes, he does.   No, he isn't.   No, he doesn't.

Henry is a taxi driver (*taxista*). Usually, he works in the morning. But today, Henry is working at night. He usually eats dinner at home. But tonight he is eating dinner in his taxi. Henry's wife works five nights a week at the hospital. She is a nurse. Tonight, Henry's children are home alone. Henry is happy because he is earning a lot of money (*está ganando mucho dinero*). But he is sad because he is not with his children.

1. Is Henry a bus driver?   No, he isn't.

2. Does Henry usually work at night?

3. Is Henry working at night now?

4. Does Henry usually eat dinner at home?

5. Is Henry eating dinner at home tonight?

6. Is Henry earning a lot of money tonight?

6.7.c Directions: Underline the gramatically correct answer.

1. Are you studying? <u>a. Yes, I am.</u> b. Yes, I do.

2. Do you like pizza? a. Yes, I am. b. Yes, I do.

3. Do you work at a restaurant? a. Yes, I am. b. Yes, I do.

4. What are you doing now? a. I relax. b. I am relaxing.

5. Does your sister speak English? a. Yes, she is. b. Yes, she does.

6. What do you do after class? a. I study. b. I am studying.

7. Are your parents playing tennis now? a. Yes, they are. b. Yes, they do.

8. When do you wash your car? a. I wash my car on Saturdays. b. I am washing my car on Saturdays.

9. What time do you go to sleep? a. I am sleeping at 11:15. b. I go to sleep at 11:15.

You use the *present progressive* tense (also called the *present continuous* tense) to talk about what you're doing right now.

The following table shows how to conjugate present progressive verbs.

I am working.	He is working.	We are working.
	She is working.	You are working.
	It is working.	They are working.

Affirmative sentences in the present progressive tense have this form:

Sujeto and the verb **to be**	Present participle (Infinitive + **ing**)	Spanish translation
He is	working.	Él está trabajando. Él trabaja.
He's	working.	

Negative sentences in the present progressive tense have this form:

Subject, the verb **to be** and **not**	Present participle (Infinitive + **ing**)	Spanish translation
He is not	working	Él no está trabajando. Él no trabaja.
He isn't	working	
He's not	working	

Yes/no questions and answers that include a present progressive verb have this form:

Yes/No questions with present progressive verbs	
Are you studying? Yes, I am. No, I am not. No, I'm not.	Are Laura and I studying? Are we studying? Yes, we are. No, we are not. No, we're not. No, we aren't.
Is Peter studying? Is he studying? Yes, he is. No, he is not. No, he isn't. No, he's not.	Are the boys studying? Are they studying? Yes, they are. No, they are not. No, they're not. No, they aren't.
Is Ana studying? Is she studying? Yes, she is. No, she is not. No, she isn't. No, she's not.	

Rules for spelling present participles:

► If a base verb ends in an **e** preceded by a consonant, create the present participle by dropping the **e** and adding **ing** (for example, **drive**, **driving**). ing
► If a base verb is one syllable and ends in a consonant preceded by a vowel, create the past participle by doubling the consonant; then adding **ing** (for example, **cut**, **cutting**).

P6.a Directions: Write the present participle of each verb.

base form	present participle	base form	present participle
1. work	working	9. write	
2. visit		10. brush	
3. drive		11. dance	
4. live		12. put	
5. carry		13. play	
6. sit		14. listen	
7. take		15. run	
8. study		16. sleep	

P6.b Directions: Look at the picture and answer each question using one of the responses below.

Yes, he is.   Yes, she is.   Yes, they are.

No, he isn't.   No, she isn't.   No, they aren't.

1. Is Luke reading?   No, he isn't.

2. Is Alex eating an apple?

3. Is Alex eating a banana?

4. Is Miguel sleeping?

5. Are Lucy and Sue sleeping?

6. Are Lucy and Sue talking?

7. Are Luke and Bev talking?

8. Is Luke writing?

9. Is Ana reading?

10. Is Mark wearing (*usar*) a hat?

P6.c Directions: Complete each question with Is or Are. Then answer the questions affirmatively, that is, start each response with Yes, followed by a short answer. Then write a long answer. Use contractions when you can.

1. __Is__ Marcos reading? 1a. __Yes, he is.__
                                          1b. __Yes, he's reading.__

2. _____ the students studying? 2a. _____
                                      2b. _____

3. _____ your parents working now? 3a. _____
                                         3b. _____

4. _____ your uncle playing soccer? 4a. _____
                                          4b. _____

P6.d Directions: Complete each question with Is or Are. Then answer the questions negatively that is, start each response with No, followed by a short answer.

1. __Is__ Amanda doing her homework? 1a. __No, she isn't.__
                                      1b. __No, she isn't doing her homework.__

2. _____ Ernesto playing video games? 2a. _____
                                            2b. _____

3. _____ Ed and Raoul playing tennis? 3a. _____
                                            3b. _____

4. _____ your aunts playing soccer? 4a. _____
                                         4b. _____

P6.e Directions: One of the sentences in each pair is not a correct sentence. Cross out the incorrect sentence.

1a. I am playing soccer.   1b. ~~I am play soccer.~~
2a. He is work now.   2b. He is working now.
3a. I am studying English.   3b. I studying English.
4a. Marcos and Ana are watch TV.   4b. Marcos and Ana are watching TV.
5a. I am not playing tennis.   5b. I no playing tennis.
6a. My boss isn't working today.   6b. My boss no working today.
7a. Lucy is washing her clothes.   7b. Lucy is wash her clothes.
8a. I walking in the park.   8b. I'm walking in the park.

P6.f Directions: Translate these sentences.

1. Estudio inglés de lunes a viernes.   I study English from Monday to Friday.

2. Estoy estudiando inglés ahora.   _____

3. Angel juega al fútból dos veces por semana. _____

4. Angel está jugando al fútbol ahora. _____

5. Sam no está hablando inglés. _____

6. Sam no habla inglés en su casa. _____

7. Estoy caminando a mi escuela ahora. _____

8. Camino a mi escuela todos los días. _____

P6.g Directions: Read the story. Then answer the questions. Use complete sentences. Use contractions when you can.

It is an unusual (*raro*) day. Armando is the only employee (*empleado*) at work. Where are the other (*otros*) employees? Angela is at home. Her daughter is sick. Angela is taking her daughter to the doctor. Ben is at home too. He is sick. Marcos is in Mexico. He is visiting his family. Ana is in San Francisco. She is at a meeting. Beatrice's car is broken (*roto*). She is taking her car to the mechanic. Armando is very busy (*ocupado*) today. He is also very tired.

1. Is Armando busy today?   Yes, he is. _____

2. Where is Angela? _____

3. What is Angela doing? _____

4. Is Ben at work today? _____

5. Is Marcos at work? _____

6. Is Marcos visiting his family? _____

7. Is Ana at a meeting in Mexico? _____

8. What is Beatrice doing? _____

9. Is Armando tired? _____

P6.h Directions: Read the conversation between two friends. Then answer the questions. Use complete sentences. Use contractions when you can.

Maria: How are you?

Luis: I'm sick.

Maria: What's wrong? (*¿Cuál es el problema?*)

Luis: I have the flu. (*la gripe*)

Maria: Do you need medicine?

Luis: Yes, I do.

Maria: What are you doing?

Luis: I'm listening to music.

Maria: OK. See you later. (*Nos vemos luego .*)

1. Where is Luis?   He's at home. _____

2. Is Luis sick? _____

3. What's wrong with Luis? _____

4. Does Luis need medicine? _____

5. What is Luis doing now? _____

Appendix A: Answers to the Exercises

Chapter 1

1.1.a **1.** boy **2.** husband **3.** television **4.** tired

1.1.b **1.** beautiful **2.** in **3.** happy **4.** black **5.** at **6.** dirty **7.** above **8.** are

1.1.c **1.** doctor **2.** white **3.** store **4.** ball **5.** pencil **6.** backpack **7.** sad **8.** happy

1.1.d **1.** cashier **2.** airplane **3.** it **4.** person **5.** apple **6.** dog **7.** above **8.** student

1.1.e **1.** on **2.** under **3.** in **4.** above

1.2.a **kitchen 1.** microwave **2.** blender **3.** refrigerator **4.** counter **5.** kitchen sink **6.** stove
living room 1. end table **2.** chair **3.** television **4.** sofa/couch **5.** coffee table **6.** picture
bedroom 1. lamp **2.** dresser **3.** night table **4.** bed
bathroom 1. mirror **2.** shower **3.** bathroom sink **4.** toilet **5.** bathtub

1.3.a **1.** behind **2.** between **3.** in front of **4.** next to

1.3.b **1b.** ~~The table is in the sofa.~~ **2b.** ~~The couch is between the end table.~~ **3b.** ~~I am on the bedroom.~~ **4a.** ~~The blender is in the counter.~~ **5b.** ~~She is next her sister.~~ **6a.** ~~I am in front my apartment.~~ **7b.** ~~The pencil is in the floor.~~ **8a.** ~~The store is between the school.~~ **9a.** ~~Your shoes are next the window.~~ **10b.** ~~The oranges are on the kitchen.~~

1.3.c **1.** The books are next to the lamp. **2.** The picture is above the sofa. **3.** My house is next to the store. **4.** My aunt is in the kitchen. **5.** Your book is between the notebook and the pen. **6.** The chairs are in front of the table. **7.** Our car is in front of the house.

1.4.a **1.** under **2.** between **3.** on **4.** on **5.** next to **6.** in front of **7.** in front of **8.** in

1.4.b **1.** Where is the ball? **2.** Where are the books? **3.** Where are the towels? **4.** Where are the socks? **5.** Where is the pizza? **6.** Where are the students?

1.5.a **1.** in **2.** at **3.** in **4.** in **5.** at **6.** at **7.** at **8.** at **9.** in **10.** in **11.** in **12.** at **13.** on **14.** in **15.** at **16.** at

1.5.b **1b.** ~~Lisa is in the beach.~~ **2a.** ~~Marian is in work.~~ **3a.** ~~Maria is in the home.~~ **4b.** ~~Our teacher is at the classroom.~~ **5b.** ~~I am at the living room.~~ **6a.** ~~The book is in the sofa.~~ **7a.** ~~My parents are at the work.~~ **8b.** ~~My friends are at the Pedros Pizza Restaurant.~~ **9b.** ~~Her house is in 8th Ave.~~ **10a.** ~~I am no at work.~~ **11a.** ~~The students are at the El Pueblo Market.~~ **12b.** ~~We are in the beach.~~

1.5.c **1.** I am in Chicago. **2.** He is in Peru. **3.** Juana is from Peru. **4.** My friends are at the beach. **5.** The students are at the library. **6.** Your books are on the bed. **7.** The toys are on the floor.

P1.a **1.** boy **2.** bed **3.** she **4.** tired **5.** green **6.** tall **7.** they **8.** happy

P1.b **1.** beautiful **2.** in **3.** bad **4.** new **5.** is **6.** dirty **7.** above **8.** we

P1.c **1.** nurse **2.** kitchen **3.** window **4.** hot **5.** pencil **6.** sick **7.** school **8.** picture

P1.d **1.** dresser **2.** rabbit **3.** on **4.** aunt **5.** children **6.** under **7.** above **8.** study

P1.e **1a.** ~~The books are next the lamp.~~ **2b.** ~~The students are on the classroom.~~ **3b.** ~~Yvonne is in the home.~~ **4a.** ~~The photos are in front the table.~~ **5b.** ~~I am at the work.~~ **6b.** ~~The dog is between the chair.~~ **7b.** ~~My wife is at the Berkeley Adult School.~~ **8a.** ~~Susan is at the Benny's Restaurant.~~

P1.f **1.** on **2.** in front of **3.** on **4.** between **5.** in **6.** under **7.** behind **8.** next to

P1.g **1.** in **2.** in **3.** at **4.** at **5.** at **6.** at **7.** at **8.** at **9.** in **10.** in **11.** on **12.** on **13.** on **14.** in **15.** at **16.** at

P1.h **1.** Your keys are on the table. **2.** My backpack is in the kitchen. **3.** Samuel is at church. **4.** The students are at the library. **5.** Your books are next to the lamp.

P1.i **1.** He is at his apartment. **2.** He is at work.

3. They are at work. **4.** They are at school. **5.** She is in her bedroom. **6.** He is at the park. **7.** They are at the park.

P1.j **1.** She is at home. **2.** She is at Silver Gym. **3.** She is at work. **4.** She is at Hoppers Restaurant. **5.** She is at school. **6.** She is at the library. **7.** She is at the supermarket. **8.** She is at home.

Chapter 2

2.1.a **1.** trabajo **2.** cita **3.** descanso **4.** fiesta **5.** reunión **6.** clase

2.1.b **1.** appointment **2.** class **3.** party **4.** meeting **5.** work **6.** break

2.1.c **1.** It is at 2 p.m. **2.** It is at 8 p.m. **3.** It is at 5:00 p.m. **4.** It is at 9 a.m. **5.** It is at 4 p.m. **6.** It is at 11 a.m.

2.1.d **1.** The meeting is at 6:00. **2.** My class is at 8:30. **3.** Your appointment is at 2:15. **4.** The party is from 9:00 to 12:00. **5.** Our appointment is from 3:00 to 4:00. **6.** My break is from 10:00 to 10:30.

2.2.a **1.** June 7, 2009 **2.** January 3, 2010 **3.** November 12, 1999 **4.** August 17, 2006 **5.** July 21, 2012 **6.** September 1, 1996

2.2.b **1.** Aug. 24, 2008 **2.** Mar. 3, 2013 **3.** Oct. 10, 2007 **4.** Dec. 1, 1999 **5.** Feb. 2, 2012 **6.** Apr. 19, 1986

2.2.c **1.** 8/17/1985 **2.** 5/7/2012 **3.** 9/11/2001 **4.** 7/16/1969 **5.** 11/25/2006 **6.** 12/25/2012

2.2.d **1.** March. **2.** Monday **3.** Friday **4.** Thursday **5.** August **6.** March **7.** Sunday **8.** Wednesday **9.** December

2.2.e **1a.** 3/3 2007 **2a.** April 4 2009 **3b.** 1-15/2010 **4a.** Feb 14 2009 **5a.** February 3 1999 **6b.** 7/17/09 **7b.** Aug 18, 2011 **8b.** 9/10 2009

2.3.a **1.** at **2.** on **3.** in **4.** in **5.** on **6.** on **7.** in **8.** at **9.** in **10.** on **11.** on **12.** in **13.** at **14.** on

2.3.b **1.** It is on January 22. **2.** It is at 1:15 p.m. **3.** It is on August 30. **4.** It is at 4:30 p.m. **5.** It is at 9 a.m. **6.** It is on March 2.

2.3.c **1.** on, at **2.** at, at **3.** in **4.** in **5.** at, in **6.** on **7.** in **8.** at, on

2.3.d **1.** to **2.** at **3.** at **4.** to **5.** from **6.** from, to

2.4.a **1.** a. 46578 **2.** a. 5/6/91 **3.** b. M. **4.** a. Puebla, Mexico **5.** c. engineer **6.** b. 816

2.4.b **1.** f **2.** h **3.** j **4.** k **5.** l **6.** a **7.** c **8.** e **9.** g **10.** i **11.** d **12.** m **13.** b **14.** n

2.4.c **1.** His last name is Montes. **2.** His street address is 2342 6th Ave. **3.** He is a construction worker. **4.** His date of birth is 8/3/87. **5.** His birthplace is Moralia, Mexico. **6.** His area code is 650. **7.** His zip code is 95014. **8.** His birthday is August 3.

2.5.a **1a.** The book of Lucy **2b.** The house of Anna **3b.** The car of Lisa **4b.** The backpack of Chris **5a.** The doctor of Mrs. Wilson. **6a.** The dog of Martin **7b.** Edgar girlfriend **8a.** The teacher of Antonio

2.5.b **1.** Antonio's book is interesting. **2.** Rodolfo's car is broken. **3.** Jackie's house is on Union Street. **4.** Alba's shoes are from Mexico. **5.** Sandra's bedroom is very clean. **6.** Juana's cousin is handsome. **7.** Pedro's father is sick. **8.** Barbara's class is interesting.

2.5.c **1.** F **2.** F **3.** T **4.** F **5.** T **6.** F

2.5.d **1.** Ana's house is pretty. Ana's house is beautiful. **2.** Ernesto's car is blue. **3.** Emily's dress is expensive. **4.** Monica's daughter is eight years old. **5.** Eva's cousin is a nurse. **6.** Nick's father is at work.

2.6.a **1a.** It is at 6:30. **2b.** No, she isn't. **3a.** It is on Mondays. **4a.** No, she isn't. **5b.** It is at our school. **6a.** It is on Thursday. **7a.** It is on Beacon Street. **8a.** It is at 2:00.

2.6.b **1.** She is at home. **2.** No, he isn't. **3.** It is at 8:00. **4.** Yes, she is. **5.** He is at the park. **6.** No, she isn't. **7.** No, she isn't. **8.** No, he isn't.

P2.a **1.** August **2.** June **3.** Saturday **4.** Monday **5.** 2010 **6.** November **7.** April **8.** Friday **9.** Friday **10.** 2014

P2.b 1. on, at 2. in 3. at, at 4. at 5. in 6. in 7. at, in 8. on 9. at 10. at, on 11. in 12. on, in

P2.c 1. from, to 2. to 3. at 4. from, to 5. from, to 6. at

P2.d 1. Where is your apartment? 2. When is your meeting? 3. What time is the party? 4. Where is your sister? 5. When is Juan's class? 6. Where is Jose's house? 7. What is your job? 8. What is her date of birth?

P2.e 1. Her last name is Ramirez. 2. Her area code is 212. 3. No, she isn't. 4. Her date of birth is 2/1/82. 5. Her birthplace is San Salvador, El Salvador. 6. No, it isn't.

P2.f 1. Lana's house is new. 2. Ken's cell phone is broken. 3. Adam's microwave is old. 4. Claudia's brother is handsome. 5. Betty's bedroom is very big. 6. Laura's car is expensive. 7. Maribel's teacher is interesting. 8. Eva's son is sick. 9. Chris' cousin is divorced. 10. Ariana's dress is beautiful.

P2.g 1. It's Tuesday. 2. Her last name is Aguilar. Juana's last name is Aguilar. 3. No, she isn't. 4. It's at 9:00. 5. It's at the clinic. 6. Yes, she is.

P2.h 1a. 3/1-2007 2b. June 22 2009 3a. 2-15/2010 4a. Dec 26, 2012 5a. February 3 1989. 6a. at morning 7b. at the afternoon 8b. at the night 9b. in 7:30 10a. at the Chavez Restaurant 11b. at the home 12a. at the Ling Pharmacy 13b. the Monday 14b. from 9:00 a 5:00

P2.i 1. Pablo's sister is pretty/beautiful. 2. Angel's car is blue. 3. The class is at 9:00. 4. The keys are in the kitchen. 5. I am in Los Angeles. 6. We are at Bruno's house. 7. My appointment is on Monday. 8. My birthday is in July. 9. Your break is from 10:00 to 10:30. 10. Your backpack is in the office.

Chapter 3

3.1.a 1. There is 2. There is 3. There are 4. There are 5. There is 6. There is

3.1.b 1b. There are a fly in your soup. 2b. There is students from Peru in my class. 3b. There are a toy on the chair. 4a. There are a dogs in the garden. 5a. There are a six children at the park. 6a. There are a TV in the kitchen. 7b.

There is two sofas in the living room. 8b. There is end table next to the couch.

3.1.c 1. There are dogs in the living room. 2. There are cats in the kitchen. 3. There are erasers in my backpack. 4. There are tables in my bedroom. 5. There are chairs in front of the sofa. 6. There are socks on the floor. 7. There are pizzas in the oven. 8. There are backpacks next to the TV.

3.1.d 1. There is a dog in the bathroom. 2. There are two bathrooms in the house. 3. There are shoes under the bed. 4. There are three pencils on the table. 5. There is a backpack next to the door.

3.2.a 1. There's a towel in the bathroom. 2. No contraction. 3. There's an orange in the kitchen. 4. There's a cat in that classroom. 5. No contraction. 6. No contraction. 7. There's a restaurant next to my school. 8. There's a ball on the floor.

3.2.b 1. They 2. There 3. There 4. They 5. They 6. There

3.2.c 1. They're 2. There are 3. There are 4. They're 5. They're 6. There are

3.2.d 1b. There're dogs in the kitchen. 2a. There're students from China in my class. 3b. There're notebooks on the table 4b. Theres a microwave in the kitchen. 5a. They is a dresser in the living room. 6a. They are two beds in the bedroom. 7b. They are a dog under the table.

3.3.a 1. There isn't a hat on the sofa. 2. There isn't a sock on the floor. 3. There isn't a jacket in the living room. 4. There isn't a coat next to the chair. 5. There aren't eggs in the kitchen. 6. There aren't shoes on the floor. 7. There aren't lamps in our bedroom. 8. There aren't pants in the dresser.

3.3.b 1. There's a hat on the bed. 2. There are socks on the bed. 3. There's a shirt on the bed. 4. There's a dress on the bed. 5. There are pants on the bed. 6. There's a jacket on the bed.

3.3.c 1. There isn't a coat on the floor.

2. There aren't jackets on the sofa. **3.** There isn't a man in front of the school. **4.** There aren't erasers in my backpack. **5.** There aren't students at the beach.

3.4.a 1a Q 1b ? 2a S 2b . 3a Q 3b ? 4a S 4b . 5a S 5b . 6a Q 6b ?

3.4.b **1.** Is there a dog in the living room? **2.** Are there dogs in the living room? **3.** Is there rice on the table? **4.** Are there maps in your classroom? **5.** Is there meat in the microwave? **6.** Is there cheese on the table? **7.** Are there students in the classroom?

3.4.c **1b.** There is a cheese on the table. **2a.** Is there a meat in the oven? **3a.** There is a rice on the floor. **4a.** There are a students from China in my class. **5b.** Is there a doctor here. **6a.** There are a dogs at the park.

3.4.d **1.** noncount **2.** noncount **3.** count **4.** count **5.** noncount **6.** count **7.** noncount **8.** count **9.** count **10.** noncount

3.5.a **1a.** Yes, there's cheese on the table. **1b.** Yes, there is. **2a.** No, there isn't a dog under the table. **2b.** No, there isn't. **3a.** No, there aren't shoes on the table. **3b.** No, there aren't. **4a.** Yes, there's a broom in front of the table. **4b.** Yes, there is. **5a.** Yes, there's a ball in front of the dog. **5b.** Yes, there is.

3.5.b **1a.** Yes, there is. **2b.** Yes, there are. **3b.** No, there aren't. **4a.** Yes, there is. **5b.** No, there aren't. **6b.** No, there isn't. **7b.** Yes, there are. **8b.** Yes, there is.

3.6.a **1a.** Yes, they are **2c.** Yes, I am. **3b.** No, they aren't. **4a.** No, there isn't. **5b.** Yes, there are. **6a.** Yes, he is. **7c.** Yes, there are. **8b.** No, they aren't.

3.6.b **1.** No, she isn't. **2.** Yes, she is. **3.** She's a nurse. **4.** Yes, she is. **5.** They're from El Salvador. **6.** Yes, there are. **7.** No, it isn't. **8.** No, there aren't. **9.** No, there aren't. **10.** Yes, they are.

P3.a **1.** There is **2.** There is **3.** There are **4.** There are **5.** There is **6.** There is

P3.b **1.** They're **2.** There **3.** There **4.** They're **5.** There **6.** There

P3.c **1.** They **2.** There **3.** They **4.** There **5.** They **6.** There

P3.d **1a.** Q **1b** ? **2a.** Q **2b** ? **3a.** S **3b** . **4a.** Q **4b** ? **5a.** Q **5b** ? **6a.** S **6b** . **7a** Q **7b** ?

P3.e **1.** Yes, she is. **2.** No, there aren't. **3.** No, there isn't. **4.** Yes, she is. **5.** No, there aren't. **6.** Yes, there is. **7.** Yes, she is.

P3.f **1a.** There is a milk in the refrigerator. **2b.** There is a cheese on the table. **3a.** There is many boys at the park. **4a.** There are meat in the kitchen. **5a.** There is a books on your dresser. **6b.** There is a engineer in our class. **7b.** There is three oranges in my backpack.

P3.g **1.** There's a pencil in my backpack. **2.** There's an apple on the table. **3.** There are apples on the table. **4.** There are four students from Peru in my class. **5.** There are two chairs in the living room. **6.** There's cheese in the refrigerator. **7.** There are pizzas in the oven. **8.** There are dogs at the park.

P3.h **1.** noncount **2.** count **3.** count **4.** noncount **5.** noncount **6.** count. **7.** noncount. **8.** count **9.** noncount **10.** noncount

P3.i **1a.** Yes, there's a cat on the floor. **1b.** Yes, there is. **2a.** Yes, there are shoes under the couch. **2b.** Yes, there are. **3a.** No, there aren't socks under the couch. **3b.** No, there aren't. **4a.** Yes, there's a lamp on the table. **4b.** Yes, there is. **5a.** No, there aren't two chairs in the living room. **5b.** No, there aren't. **6a.** Yes, there's a window in the living room. **6b.** Yes, there is. **7a.** No, there isn't a table in front of the couch. **7b.** No, there isn't.

Chapter 4

4.1.a **1.** trabajar **2.** jugar **3.** comer **4.** vivir **5.** hablar **6.** sentir **7.** lavar **8.** caminar **9.** manejar **10.** tener

4.1.b **1.** drive **2.** work **3.** wash **4.** play **5.** eat **6.** like. **7.** live. **8.** have **9.** feel **10.** speak

4.1.c **1.** <u>Antonio</u> <u>walks</u> to school. **2.** <u>Ana</u> <u>feels</u> sad. **3.** <u>Lucas</u> <u>is</u> from Mexico. **4.** <u>I</u> <u>speak</u> English.

5. <u>Jose</u> and <u>I</u> <u>are</u> in love. **6.** <u>Joe and Ana</u> <u>play</u> soccer at the park. **7.** <u>Andres and Lisa</u> <u>have</u> a new baby. **8.** <u>Luis</u> <u>drives</u> a beautiful car. **9.** <u>We</u> <u>like</u> pizza. **10.** <u>They</u> <u>work</u> at Bobos Restaurant. **11.** <u>Paola</u> <u>speaks</u> Chinese. **12.** <u>Ana</u> <u>feels</u> tired. **13.** <u>I</u> <u>have</u> two dogs. **14.** <u>Andres</u> <u>lives</u> in Los Angeles. **15.** <u>Maria</u> <u>speaks</u> Spanish. **16.** <u>Peter and James</u> <u>like</u> Chinese food.

4.1.d **1.** N **2.** A **3.** A **4.** V **5.** V **6.** A **7.** N **8.** V **9.** V **10.** N **11.** A **12.** N **13.** V **14.** V **15.** N **16.** N **17.** N **18.** N **19.** A **20.** N **21.** A **22.** V **23.** N **24.** V

4.1.e. **1.** bed **2.** Andrew **3.** new **4.** ball **5.** car **6.** house.

4.2.a. **1.** work **2.** works **3.** work **4.** work **5.** works **6.** work

4.2.b. **1.** lives **2.** live **3.** live **4.** live **5.** live **6.** lives

4.2.c. **1.** like **2.** like **3.** like **4.** like **5.** likes **6.** likes

4.2.d **1.** play **2.** lives **3.** eat **4.** speak **5.** work **6.** live **7.** walk **8.** eat **9.** speaks **10.** works **11.** play **12.** like **13.** lives **14.** eats **15.** feel **16.** drives **17.** feels **18.** walk

4.2.e **1b.** ~~I plays soccer.~~ **2a.** ~~He live in a big house.~~ **3b.** ~~I likes watermelon.~~ **4a.** ~~He feel sad.~~ **5b.** ~~We works in Chicago.~~ **6b.** ~~You walks to school.~~ **7b.** ~~She play tennis.~~ **8a.** ~~I walks in the park.~~ **9b.** ~~They works at a restaurant.~~

4.3.a **1.** he **2.** she **3.** they **4.** she **5.** they **6.** we **7.** it **8.** we **9.** he **10.** it **11.** they **12.** they

4.3.b **1.** lives **2.** lives **3.** live **4.** live **5.** live **6.** lives

4.3.c **1.** likes **2.** likes **3.** like **4.** likes **5.** like **6.** likes

4.3.d **1.** speaks **2.** speaks **3.** speak **4.** speak **5.** speak **6.** speaks

4.3.e **1.** plays **2.** live **3.** eat **4.** feels **5.** works **6.** plays **7.** like **8.** feel **9.** work **10.** plays

4.3.f **1.** The students live in Hawaii. **2.** My mother feels happy. **3.** I walk in the park. **4.** Marian and Marcos live in Guadalajara. **5.** Lisa works at Fries Restaurant.

4.4.a **1a.** ~~I am study English.~~ **2a.** ~~They are like the United States.~~ **3a.** ~~Susan she is likes soccer.~~ **4b.** ~~I am driver to work.~~ **5b.** ~~You are work today.~~ **6b.** ~~I feeling sad.~~ **7b.** ~~I playing volleyball with my friends.~~ **8a.** ~~I driving to work.~~ **9a.** ~~I having two jobs.~~ **10a.** ~~My friend is lives in Chicago.~~

4.4.b **1.** plays **2.** live **3.** eat **4.** feels **5.** speaks **6.** live **7.** walks **8.** drive **9.** plays **10.** like **11.** like **12.** work **13.** play **14.** drives **15.** play **16.** feel

4.4.c **1.** The engineers <u>work</u> eight hours a day. **2.** I <u>go</u> to class at 2:00. **3.** The children <u>watch</u> television at 3:30. **4.** I <u>study</u> in the kitchen. **5.** Ernesto <u>works</u> at a restaurant. **6.** I <u>have</u> two sisters. **7.** We <u>like</u> Chinese food. **8.** Ana <u>feels</u> sick today. **9.** We <u>live</u> in Seattle. **10.** I <u>eat</u> breakfast at work.

4.5.a **1.** fixes **2.** watches **3.** studies **4.** relaxes **5.** speaks **6.** pays **7.** brushes **8.** writes **9.** carries **10.** feels **11.** plays **12.** listens

4.5.b **1.** carries **2.** study **3.** watches **4.** play **5.** watch **6.** studies **7.** brush **8.** drive **9.** drives **10.** have **11.** brushes **12.** carry

4.5.c **1.** good **2.** cheap **3.** hospital **4.** hair **5.** ball **6.** English **7.** car **8.** happy

4.6.a **1.** have **2.** has **3.** has **4.** has **5.** has **6.** have **7.** has **8.** have **9.** have **10.** have

4.6.b **1.** go **2.** goes **3.** go **4.** goes **5.** go **6.** go **7.** go **8.** goes **9.** go **10.** go

4.6.c **1.** speaks **2.** goes **3.** studies **4.** has **5.** watches **6.** listens **7.** writes **8.** does **9.** works **10.** relaxes **11.** reads **12.** fixes

4.6.d Her name is Ana Banks. She lives in Los Angeles. She has a job. She works at Celia's Restaurant. She is a cashier. She likes her job. She drives to her job. She also studies English. Her class is on Tuesday and Thursday from 7 p.m. to 9 p.m.

4.7.a **1.** She gets up at 6 a.m. **2.** She takes a shower at 6:10 a.m. **3.** She eats breakfast at 6:20 a.m. **4.** She walks to work at 7 a.m. **5.** She eats lunch at 11:30 a.m. **6.** She watches television at 4 p.m. **7.** She prepares dinner at 5:30 p.m. **8.** She goes to class at 7 p.m. **9.** She goes to bed at 10:30 p.m.

4.7.b Las respuestas varían según el estudiante.

4.7.c **1.** F. **2.** T. **3.** F. **4.** T. **5.** F **6.** T

4.8.a **1.** I often drink milk. **2.** I always watch TV. **3.** I sometimes play soccer. **4.** I usually eat meat for dinner. **5.** My boss never speaks English. **6.** My teacher usually speaks English. **7.** Amanda's husband never drives to work. **8.** We often listen to music. **9.** My parents never eat Chinese food. **10.** The students sometimes walk to school.

4.8.b Las respuestas varían según el estudiante.

4.8.c 1b. ~~I play soccer never.~~ 2b. ~~I take a shower at night usually.~~ 3a. ~~My sister does always her homework.~~ 4a. ~~Luisa cooks sometimes dinner.~~ 5a. ~~My sister studies sometimes English.~~ 6a. ~~My daughter walks always to school.~~ 7b. ~~Luke eats dinner usually at home.~~ 8a. ~~The boys play soccer never on the weekends.~~ 9a. ~~I feel tired always after work.~~ 10b. ~~My dog sleeps on my bed usually.~~

4.9.a **1.** I drink soda once a week. **2.** Lionel watches TV five days a week. **3.** Luke plays volleyball every day. **4.** Peter does his homework five days a week. **5.** The students go to the library every day. **6.** Magali goes to church three times a week. **7.** The children eat pizza twice a month. **8.** I go to the beach once a year.

4.9.b Las respuestas varían según el estudiante.

4.9.c 1b. ~~I brush twice a day my teeth.~~ 2b. ~~I call once a week my family.~~ 3b. ~~We five days a week work.~~ 4a. ~~The students go to the library five day a week.~~ 5a. ~~My aunt and uncle every year visit Mexico.~~

4.9.d **1.** I work five days a week. **2.** Lucas works six days a week. **3.** I go to Dallas once a week. **4.** My uncle goes to Los Angeles once a month. **5.** Ernesto visits Mexico twice a year.

P4.a **1.** N **2.** A **3.** A **4.** V **5.** N **6.** A **7.** N **8.** N **9.** A **10.** V **11.** A **12.** V **13.** V **14.** N **15.** N **16.** V **17.** N **18.** N **19.** A **20.** N **21.** N **22.** V **23.** V **24.** V

P4.b **1.** work **2.** lives **3.** like **4.** speak **5.** play **6.** has **7.** go **8.** eat **9.** finishes **10.** watches **11.** live **12.** brush **13.** study **14.** works **15.** takes **16.** drive **17.** like **18.** takes **19.** eat **20.** feels **21.** drives **22.** go **23.** needs **24.** study **25.** work **26.** eat **27.** has **28.** go

P4.c **1.** speaks **2.** brushes **3.** has **4.** fixes **5.** carries **6.** relaxes **7.** studies **8.** writes **9.** finishes **10.** reads **11.** does **12.** takes **13.** feels **14.** makes

P4.d Her name is Liliana Garcia. She lives in Dallas, Texas. She is a student. She studies English and math. She goes to Mathews Community College. She also has a job. She is an engineer. She works in a large office. She fixes computers. She likes her job.

P4.e **1.** F **2.** T **3.** F **4.** T **5.** F **6.** F **7.** T **8.** T **9.** F **10.** F **11.** T **12.** F

P4.f 1b. ~~I likes soccer.~~ 2b. ~~I needs a job.~~ 3a. ~~Angela like watermelon.~~ 4a. ~~Our living room haves two sofas.~~ 5a. ~~My sister study English two nights a week.~~ 6a. ~~My daughter walk to school.~~ 7b. ~~The boys plays tennis twice a week.~~ 8a. ~~Julio study English at home.~~

P4.g **1.** I drink coffee once a week. **2.** Pat goes to the gym twice a month. **3.** Phyillis works six days a week. **4.** I wash clothes twice a week. **5.** The students go to the museum once a month. **6.** Leo goes to the beach twice a year.

P4.h Las respuestas varían según el estudiante.

P4.i **1.** I never go to San Francisco. **2.** I always drink coffee in the morning. **3.** My daughter has two jobs. **4.** Ana washes her clothes once a week. **5.** My mother goes to Chicago twice a year. **6.** I work five days a week. **7.** My boss always speaks English. **8.** The students usually walk to school.

Chapter 5

5.1.a **1.** N. **2.** A **3.** N **4.** A **5.** N **6.** A **7.** A **8.** N **9.** N **10.** N

5.1.b **1.** I do not have a big family. **2.** I do not have a job. **3.** I do not need a job. **4.** I do not like your shirt. **5.** The women do not work on

Tuesdays. **6.** The children do not play soccer once a week. **7.** They do not study English at the university. **8.** We do not get up early.

5.1.c **1.** I do not have a big house. **2.** I do not speak English. **3.** I do not study Spanish. **4.** You do not speak Italian. **5.** We do not need a new sofa. **6.** She does not walk to school. **7.** They do not live in Los Angeles.

5.1.d **1a.** I no have a job. **2b.** They not work at Bo's Restaurant. **3a.** We no like Chinese food. **4a.** I not work on the weekends. **5a.** My parents do not living in Canada. **6a.** I no go to bed at 10:00. **7b.** My wife no work on Saturdays.

5.2.a **1.** Alba does not live in Seattle. **2.** Peter does not live in Washington D.C. **3.** My teacher does not live in Florida. **4.** I do not live in Canada. **5.** We do not live in Boston. **6.** Susan does not speak Spanish. **7.** Ana does not get up early. **8.** Juan does not like Jennifer Lopez. **9.** We do not work in Seattle. **10.** The teachers do not drive to work.

5.2.b **1.** Louisa does not live in Chicago. **2.** Mario does not live in New York. **3.** Angela does not live in Salem. **4.** Bruce and Elizabeth do not live in Paris. **5.** We do not live in Seattle. **6.** My brother does not live in Mexico. **7.** I do not study English at the university. **8.** Armando does not study French. **9.** Lucy does not study English. **10.** I do not play soccer at the park.

5.2.c **1b.** She do not live in Havana. **2a.** Louisa no living in Canada. **3a.** My sister does not lives in Honduras. **4b.** Patricia does no study English. **5a.** My mother not does work at the hospital. **6b.** Raymundo no like his apartment. **7b.** Alana no is wash her clothes at the laundromat. **8a.** Laura no feel sick today.

5.3.a **1.** does not have **2.** does not go **3.** do not have **4.** does not do **5.** do not speak **6.** do not have **7.** do not go **8.** does not feel **9.** does not have

5.3.b Las respuestas varían según el estudiante.

5.3.c Andrew does not have a good life. He does not have a good job. He does not work. He does not go to the mall. He does not go to the park to play soccer. He does not go dancing. He does

not have a good family. He does not have nice friends.

5.3.d **1.** I do not have a dog. **2.** Elena does not have a cat. **3.** We do not have a big house. **4.** The students do not have a good teacher. **5.** I do not go to San Francisco on Saturdays. **6.** I do not do my homework.

5.4.a **1a.** Martha does not work five days a week. **1b.** Martha doesn't work five days a week. **2a.** My sister does not live in Panama. **2b.** My sister doesn't live in Panama. **3a.** Gabriela and Andrew do not eat dinner at home on Saturdays. **3b.** Gabriela and Andrew don't eat dinner at home on Saturdays. **4a.** Julio does not speak Italian. **4b.** Julio doesn't speak Italian. **5a.** I do not like cheese. **5b.** I don't like cheese. **6a.** I do not have a small kitchen. **6b.** I don't have a small kitchen.

5.4.b **1.** F **2.** F **3.** T **4.** F **5.** T **6.** F **7.** T **8.** F

5.5.a **1.** isn't **2.** don't **3.** isn't **4.** doesn't **5.** don't **6.** don't **7.** aren't **8.** doesn't **9.** aren't **10.** don't

5.5.b **1.** I don't live in Hawaii. **2.** We don't have a dog. **3.** I'm not tired. **4.** She doesn't work at a restaurant. **5.** Juana doesn't need a car. **6.** Her garden isn't beautiful. **7.** The cooks aren't tired. **8.** We don't study English every day. **9.** My son doesn't have a good teacher. **10.** Andrea isn't my cousin.

5.5.c I'm not happy. I don't like my job. My job isn't interesting. I don't have enough money. I am not in love with my husband. I don't live in a nice house. I don't have a yard. I don't like my life.

5.5.d **1a.** I no living in Texas. **2b.** Louisa doesn't a doctor. **3b.** My brother isn't has a job. **4b.** Patricia no is student. **5a.** My father no is work at that restaurant. **6a.** We no like Chinese food. **7b.** The laundromat doesn't is closed. **8a.** We don't aren't married.

5.6.a **1a.** Q **1b.** ? **2a.** Q **2b.** ? **3a.** S **3b.** . **4a.** S **4b.** . **5a.** S **5b.** . **6a.** Q **6b.** ? **7a.** Q **7b.** ? **8a.** Q **8b.** ?

5.6.b **1.** Do you work? **2.** Do you speak English? **3.**

Do you like apples? **4.** Do you live in Canada? **5.** Do you need a car? **6.** Do you play soccer? **7.** Does Ana speak Spanish? **8.** Does Jose live here?

5.6.c **1a.** Do **1b.** No, they don't. **2a.** Do **2b.** No, they don't. **3a.** Do **3b.** No, they don't. **4a.** Does **4b.** Yes, she does. **5a.** Does **5b.** Yes, he does. **6a.** Do **6b.** Yes, they do. **7a.** Do **7b.** Yes, they do.

5.7.a **1a.** Yes, she does. **2b.** Yes, I do. **3a.** Yes, he does. **4b.** No, they don't. **5a.** No, she doesn't. **6a.** No, she doesn't. **7b.** Yes, she does. **8a.** No, I don't.

5.7.b **1a.** Yes, I do. **1b.** Yes, I like pizza. **2a.** Yes, I do. **2b.** Yes, I work at a restaurant. **3a.** Yes, she does. **3b.** Yes, she lives in the U.S. **4a.** Yes, they do. **4b.** Yes, they speak English.

5.7.c **1a.** No, I don't. **1b.** No, I don't have a job. **2a.** No, I don't. **2b.** No, I don't like American food. **3a.** No, he doesn't. **3b.** No, he doesn't live in Mexico. **4a.** No, it doesn't. **4b.** No, it doesn't have a microwave.

5.8.a Las respuestas varían según el estudiante.

5.8.b **1.** No, he isn't. **2.** Yes, he does. **3.** No, he doens't. **4.** Yes, he is. **5.** Yes, he does. **6.** Yes, he does. **7.** No, he isn't. **8.** Yes, he does. **9.** Yes, he is. **10.** Yes, he does. **11.** No, he doesn't. **12.** Yes, he is.

5.9.a **1.** Where do you study English? **2.** When do you study English? **3.** When do you call your family? **4.** What time do they eat dinner? **5.** Where does Luis work? **6.** Where does Julia live?

5.9.b **1a.** She works from Monday to Friday. **2b.** I play soccer on Tuesdays. **3b.** I study English from 8 to 10 p.m. **4a.** I buy food at Andres Market. **5a.** She eats lunch at Max's Cafe. **6a.** It starts at 9:00. **7a.** She studies at San Juan Adult School. **8a.** I wash my car on Saturdays.

5.9.c **1.** He gets up at 9:00. **2.** No, he doesn't. **3.** He eats breakfast at Charley's Restaurant. **4.** He drinks a cup of coffee. **5.** He goes to the park in the afternoon. **6.** He walks in the park. **7.** Yes, he does. **8.** He goes to sleep at 11:00.

P5.a **1.** Lisa doesn't drive to work. **2.** Mario doesn't go to Atlas Community College. **3.** I don't play soccer on Mondays. **4.** The students don't have homework every day. **5.** We don't live in Seattle. **6.** My brother doesn't live in Mexico. **7.** I don't work at a restaurant. **8.** My parents don't like Chinese food. **9.** I'm not tired. **10.** I don't eat lunch at 11:30. **11.** They don't watch television every night. **12.** Jose isn't my uncle. **13.** My husband doesn't want a dog. **14.** Mary and Justin don't have two daughters. **15.** You're not late./ You aren't late.

P5.b **1.** doesn't have **2.** doesn't go **3.** doesn't have **4.** doesn't go **5.** doesn't have **6.** doesn't do **7.** doesn't have **8.** don't go **9.** do not **10.** do not **11.** don't have **12.** doesn't **13.** am not **14.** does not

P5.c Responses depend on the student.

P5.d **1.** No, they don't. **2.** No, she isn't. **3.** Yes, they do. **4.** No, she doesn't. **5.** Yes, she does. **6.** Yes, she does. **7.** No, she doesn't. **8.** Yes, she does. **9.** Yes, she does. **10.** No, she doesn't. **11.** Yes, they are. **12.** Yes, they do.

P5.e **1.** Where do you work? **2.** When do you work? **3.** Where does Lucy buy shoes? **4.** Where does Ana play soccer? **5.** What time do you eat lunch? **6.** When does Jose work?

P5.f **1a.** Yes, she does. **2a.** Yes, I am. **3a.** Yes, she is. **4b.** No, they don't. **5a.** Yes, they are. **6b.** No, he doesn't. **7a.** No, she doesn't. **8b.** Yes, she does. **9a.** No, I don't. **10b.** No, she doesn't.

P5.g **1.** I don't have a car. **2.** My daughter isn't a nurse. She's a doctor. **3.** My mother doesn't live in Houston. She lives in Atlanta. **4.** I have two jobs. **5.** My sisters don't speak English. **6.** My kitchen isn't big. It's small. **7.** My husband doesn't want a dog. **8.** I'm not happy because I don't have a car. **9.** My daughter doesn't like pizza. **10.** My friends aren't at the park. They're at school.

P5.h **1.** Do you have a car? **2.** Do you speak English? **3.** Do you live in Chicago? **4.** Do you feel sick? **5.** Do you work at Pop's Pizza? **6.** Does your sister have a car? **7.** Does your brother speak English? **8.** Does Liliana live in Miami?

Chapter 6

6.1.a 1. talking 2. working 3. eating 4. playing 5. going 6. doing 7. brushing 8. cleaning

6.1.b 1. am sleeping 2. are sleeping 3. is sleeping 4. is sleeping 5. is sleeping 6. are sleeping 7. is sleeping 8. is sleeping 9. are sleeping 10. are sleeping 11. are sleeping 12. is sleeping

6.1.c 1. am working 2. are working 3. is working 4. is working 5. is working 6. are working 7. is working 8. is working 9. is working 10. are working 11. are working 12. are working

6.1.d 1. are reading 2. are reading 3. is reading 4. is reading 5. am reading 6. are reading 7. is reading 8. is reading

6.2.a 1. fixing 2. watching 3. studying 4. relaxing 5. speaking 6. paying 7. going 8. sitting 9. brushing 10. writing 11. carrying 12. putting 13. playing 14. listening 15. running 16. driving

6.2.b 1. is preparing 2. are driving 3. are watching 4. is taking 5. am brushing 6. are speaking 7. am cutting 8. are playing

6.2.c 1. I am reading a book. 2. Susan is dancing. 3. Irma is watching television. 4. We are studying English. 5. The girls are sleeping. 6. Lillian is working and Lucas is at school.

6.3.a 1. I am not working. 2. They are not watching television. 3. She is not reading. 4. We are not driving home from work. 5. It is not raining. 6. They are not running in the park. 7. He is not preparing lunch. 8. I am not talking to my sister. 9. We are not walking to the mall.

6.3.b 1. I <u>am studying</u> Spanish. 2. The students <u>are playing</u> soccer. 3. We <u>are not working</u> now. 4. The children <u>are playing</u> at the park. 5. They <u>are reading</u> now. 6. Laura <u>is sitting</u> in the kitchen. 7. Antonio <u>is sleeping</u> now. 8. My parents <u>are not visiting</u> my sister. 9. I <u>am not sleeping</u>. 10. They <u>are not talking</u>.

6.3.c 1. I am not working now. 2. I am not studying now. 3. Marlene is not sleeping. 4. The children are not playing now. 5. My father is not eating.

6.4.a 1. I'm reading. 2. They're playing soccer. 3. She's working. 4. We're walking to work. 5. It's raining. 6. They're carrying their books. 7. He's repairing his car. 8. I'm taking a shower.

6.4.b 1. She isn't working today. / She's not working today. 2. They aren't brushing their teeth. / They're not brushing their teeth. 3. She isn't taking a shower. / She's not taking a shower. 4. We aren't visiting your parents. / We're not visiting your parents. 5. It isn't raining. / It's not raining. 6. He isn't sitting in his car. / He's not sitting in his car. 7. He isn't talking to his girlfriend. / He's not talking to his girlfriend. 8. I'm not playing the violin.

6.4.c 1. <u>I am studying</u> French. 2. They <u>are working</u> at an airport. 3. We <u>are not working</u> six days a week. 4. He <u>is not walking</u> to school. 5. They <u>are not listening</u> to music. 6. We <u>are reading</u> in the kitchen. 7. She <u>is not sleeping</u> now. 8. I <u>am visiting</u> my daughter in Colorado.

6.5.a 1. Are--No, they aren't. 2. Is--No, he isn't. 3. Is--Yes, she is. 4. Is--Yes, she is. 5. Are--No, they aren't. 6. Are--No, they aren't. 7. Are--Yes, they are. 8. Is--Yes, he is. 9. Is--No, he isn't. 10. Is--Yes, she is. 11. Is--No, she isn't.

6.5.b 1. Are you working? 2. Is Juana working now? 3. Are you going home? 4. Is Caroline studying now? 5. Are they at home? 6. Is Ernesto eating dinner? 7. Are you sleeping? 8. Does Jose live here?

6.6.a 1. She's reading. 2. He's writing. 3. They're eating. 4. He's drinking. 5. They're talking. 6. He's sleeping.

6.6.b 1. e 2. b 3. f 4. c 5. d 6. a 7. h 8. g

6.6.c 1. What are you doing? 2. Where are you going? 3. Why are you crying? 4. What is

Alberto doing? **5.** Where is he going?

6.7.a 1. am studying, present progressive
2. studies, simple present 3. know, simple present 4. works, simple present 5. has, simple present 6. am watching, present progressive 7. watch, simple present 8. are listening, present progressive

6.7.b 1. No, he isn't. 2. No, he doesn't. 3. Yes, he is. 4. Yes, he does. 5. No, he isn't. 6. Yes, he is.

6.7.c 1a. Yes, I am. 2b. Yes, I do. 3b. Yes, I do. 4b. I am relaxing. 5b. Yes, she does. 6a. I study. 7a. Yes, they are. 8a. I wash my car on Saturdays. 9b. I go to sleep at 11:15.

P6.a 1. working 2. visiting 3. driving 4. living 5. carrying 6. sitting 7. taking 8. studying 9. writing 10. brushing 11. dancing 12. putting 13. playing 14. listening 15. running 16. sleeping

P6.b 1. No, he isn't. 2. No, he isn't. 3. Yes, he is. 4. Yes, he is. 5. No, they aren't. 6. Yes, they are. 7. No, they aren't. 8. Yes, he is. 9. Yes, she is. 10. Yes, he is.

P6.c 1. Is 1a. Yes, he is. 1b. Yes, he's reading. 2. Are 2a. Yes, they are. 2b Yes, they're studying. 3. Are 3a. Yes, they are. 3b. Yes, they're working now. 4. Is 4a. Yes, he is. 4b. Yes, he's playing soccer.

P6.d 1. Is 1a. No, she isn't./No, she's not. 1b. No, she isn't doing her homework./No, she's not doing her homework. 2. Is 2a. No, he isn't. No, he's not. 2b. No, he isn't playing video games. / No, he's not playing video games. 3. Are 3a. No, they aren't. / No, they're not. 3b. No, they aren't playing tennis. / No, they're not playing tennis. 4. Are 4a. No, they're not. / No they aren't. 4b. No, they're not playing soccer. / No, they aren't playing soccer.

P6.e 1b. ~~I am play soccer.~~ 2a. ~~He is work now.~~ 3b. ~~I studying English.~~ 4a. ~~Marcos and Ana are watch TV.~~ 5b. ~~I no playing tennis.~~ 6b. ~~My boss no working today.~~ 7b. ~~Lucy is wash her clothes.~~ 8a. ~~I walking in the park.~~

P6.f 1. I study English from Monday to Friday.

2. I'm studying English now. 3. Angel plays soccer twice a week. 4. Angel is playing soccer now. 5. Sam isn't speaking English. 6. Sam doesn't speak English at home. 7. I'm walking to my school now. 8. I walk to my school every day.

P6.g 1. Yes he is. 2. She's at home. 3. She's taking her daughter to the doctor. 4. No, he isn't. 5. No, he isn't. 6. Yes, he is. 7. No, she isn't. 8. She is taking her car to the mechanic. 9. Yes, he is.

P6.h 1. He's at home. 2. Yes, he is. 3. He has the flu. 4. Yes, he does. 5. He's listening to music.

Appendix B: Contractions with *To be*

The following table shows how to conjugate affirmative sentences with the verb **to be**.

Affirmative sentences without contractions	Affirmative sentences with contractions	Spanish translation
I am tired.	I'm tired.	Estoy cansado. Estoy cansada.
You are tired.	You're tired.	Estás cansado. Estás cansada.
He is tired.	He's tired.	Él está cansado.
She is tired.	She's tired.	Ella está cansada.
It is tired.	It's tired.	
We are tired.	We're tired.	Nosotros estamos cansados. Nosotras estamos cansadas.
They are tired.	They're tired.	Ellos están cansadas. Ellas están cansados.

The following table shows how to conjugate negative sentences with the verb **to be**. Notice that, with the exception of **I**, there are two contractions to choose from for each subject pronoun. Both contractions mean the same thing.

Negative sentences without contractions	Negative sentences with contractions	Spanish translation
I am not tired.	I'm not tired.	No estoy cansado. No estoy cansada.
You are not tired.	You're not tired. You aren't tired.	No estás cansado. No estás cansada.
He is not tired.	He's not tired. He isn't tired.	Él no está cansado.
She is not tired.	She's not tired. She isn't tired.	Ella no está cansada.
It is not tired.	It's not tired. It isn't tired.	
We are not tired.	We're not tired. We aren't tired.	Nosotros no estamos cansados. Nosotras no estamos cansadas.
They are not tired.	They're not tired. They aren't tired.	Ellos no están cansados. Ellas no están cansadas.

Glossary

adjective: A word that modifies or describes a noun or pronoun. **Handsome** (guapo), **pretty** (bonita) and **blue** (azul) are examples of adjectives.

adverb: A word that describes an adjective, verb or other adverb. **Always** and **very** are examples of adverbs.

adverb of frequency: An adverb that tells how often something occurs. **Always** and **sometimes** are adverbs of frequency.

auxiliary verb: A verb that helps the main verb. **Do** and **does** are auxiliary verbs.

base verb: A verb that is helped by an auxiliary verb. In this sentence, **I do not like pizza, like** is the base verb. Also called *main verb*.

contraction: A word that is formed by combining two other words. **Al** and **del** are contractions in Spanish. **I'm** and **isn't** are examples of contractions in English.

demonstrative adjective: An adjective that points out whether something is near by or far away. In English, the demonstrative adjectives are **this**, **that**, **these** and **those**.

gender: A type of classification that defines nouns, pronouns and adjectives as masculine, feminine or neuter. **Casa** is a feminine noun; **techo** is a masculine noun. In English, gender only applies to a few nouns such as **mother** and **father**.

main verb: A verb that is helped by an auxiliary verb. In this sentence, **I do not like pizza, like** is the main verb. Also called *base verb*.

noun: A person, place, animal or thing. **Teacher** (maestra), **book** (libro) and **park** (parque) are examples of nouns.

plural noun: A noun that refers to more than one person, place, animal, or thing. **Books** (libros) is an example of a plural noun.

possessive adjective: An adjective that shows that something belongs to or is related to a noun. **My** (mi, mis) is an example of a possessive adjective.

possessive noun: A word that is used to show that something belongs to someone or something else. For example, in the sentence **Juana's sofa is new**, **Juana's** is the possessive noun because it shows that the sofa belongs to Juana.

preposition: A word that describes time, place, direction, or location. **Over** (arriba de) and **next to** (al lado de) are prepositions.

present continuous: A verb tense that is used to talk about activities that are happening right now. Also called *present continuous*. For example, **I am working now.**

present progressive: A verb tense that is used to talk about activities that are happening right now. Also called *present progressive*. For example, **I am working now.**

pronoun: A word that takes the place of a noun. (See *subject pronoun*)

question word: A word that often is included in a question. Common question words in English are **who**, **what**, **when**, **where**, **why**, **how**, and **how many**.

simple present: A verb tense that is used to talk about habitual activities that occur in the present. For example. **I work five days a week.**

singular noun: A noun that refers to one person, place, animal or thing. **Book** (libro) is an example of a singular noun.

subject pronoun: A pronoun that is the subject of a sentence. In English, the subject pronouns are **I**, **you**, **he**, **she**, **it**, **we** and **they**.

subject: The word or words in the sentence that tell who or what the sentence is about. The subject is usually the first noun or pronoun in the sentence.

verb: A word that shows action or state of being. **To be** (ser and estar) and to **have** (tener) are the most common verbs. Other examples of verbs are **talk**, **sing**, **play** and **study**.

verb tense: The form of the verb that tells whether the verb occurs in the past, present or future.

Index

English/Spanish Dictionary

A

above (*abóv*)	arriba de
age (*éish*)	edad
airplane (*érplein*)	avión
alone (*alóun*)	solo, sola
also (*ólsou*)	también
always (*ólweis*)	siempre
am (*am*)	soy, estoy
an (*an*)	un, una
and (*and*)	y
apple (*apl*)	manzana
appointment (*apóintment*)	cita
April (*éiprel*)	abril
architect (*árquetect*)	arquitecto(a)
are (*ar*)	eres, somos, son, estás, estamos, están
area code (*érea cóud*)	código de área
artist (*ártist*)	artista
at (*at*)	a, en
August (*ógost*)	agosto
aunt (*ant*)	tía

B

baby (*béibi*)	bebé(a)
babysitter (*béibisiter*)	niñera
backpack (*bákpak*)	mochila
bad (*bad*)	malo(a)
bag (*bag*)	bolsa
ball (*bol*)	pelota
bathroom (*bázrrum*)	baño
bathtub (*báztab*)	tina, bañera
be (verb) (*bi*)	ser, estar
beach (*bich*)	playa
beautiful (*biútiful*)	hermoso(a)
because (*bicós*)	porque
bed (*bed*)	cama
before (*bifór*)	antes
begin (*biguín*)	empezar
behind (*biháind*)	detrás
better (*béter*)	mejor
between (*bituín*)	**entre**
big (*big*)	grande
birth (*berz*)	nacimiento
birthday (*bérzdei*)	cumpleaños
birthplace (*berzpléis*)	lugar de nacimiento
black (*blak*)	negro(a)
blender (*blénder*)	licuadora
blouse (*bláus*)	blusa
blue (*blu*)	azul
book (*buk*)	libro
boss (*bos*)	jefe(a)

box (*box*)	caja
boy (*bói*)	niño
boyfriend (*bóifrend*)	novio
bread (*bred*)	pan
break (*bréik*)	descanso
breakfast (*brékfast*)	desayuno
broken (*bróuken*)	roto(a)
broom (*brum*)	escoba
brother (*bráder*)	hermano
brother-in-law (*bráder in loh*)	cuñado
brown (*bráun*)	café, marrón, castaño
brush (*brash*)	cepillar
busy (*bisi*)	ocupado, ocupada
buy (*bái*)	comprar

C

call (*col*)	llamar
car (*car*)	carro, coche, auto
carpenter (*cárpenter*)	carpintero
carry (*kérri*)	llevar, cargar
cashier (*cashíer*)	cajero(a)
cat (*cat*)	gato(a)
chair (*cher*)	silla
cheap (*chip*)	barato(a)
cheese (*chis*)	queso
cherry (*chérri*)	cereza
child (*cháild*)	niño(a)
church (*cherch*)	iglesia
city (*síti*)	ciudad
class (*clas*)	clase
classroom (*clásrrum*)	aula, sala de clase
clean (*clin*)	limpio(a)
clothes (*clóuds*)	ropa
coat (*cóut*)	abrigo
code (*cóud*)	código
coffee (*cófi*)	café
coffee table (*cófi téibl*)	mesa de café
cold (**adj.**) (*cóuld*)	frío(a)
cold (**noun**) (*cóuld*)	frío, resfriado
color (*cólor*)	color
company (*cómpani*)	compañía
complete (*complít*)	completo(a)

D

dark (*dark*)	oscuro(a)
date (*déit*)	fecha
date of birth (*déit of berz*)	fecha de nacimiento
daughter (*dóter*)	hija

daughter-in-law *(dóter in loh)* nuera

day *(déi)* día
December *(dicémber)* diciembre
dictionary *(díkshonari)* diccionario
dinner *(díner)* cena

E

eat *(it)* comer
egg *(eg)* huevo
eight *(éit)* ocho
eighteen *(éitin)* dieciocho
eighty *(éiti)* ochenta
eleven *(iléven)* once
employee *(impló-i)* empleado
end table *(end téibl)* mesita auxiliar
engineer *(inshenír)* ingeniero(a)
eraser *(irréiser)* borrador
evening *(ívnin)*
expensive *(expénsif)* caro(a)
eye *(ái)* ojo

F

father *(fáder)* padre
father-in-law *(fáder in loh)* suegro
fear *(fir)* miedo
feet *(fit)* pies
fifteen *(fíftin)* quince
fifty *(fífti)* cincuenta
first *(ferst)* primero(a)
first name *(ferst néim)* primer nombre
five *(fáiv)* cinco
foot *(fut)* pie
forty *(fórti)* cuarenta
four *(for)* cuatro
fourteen *(fórtin)* catorce
friend *(frend)* amigo(a)
from *(from)* de, desde

G

garden *(gárdn)* jardín
gardener *(gárdner)* jardinero(a)
girl *(guerl)* niña
girlfriend *(guérlfrend)* novia
good *(gud)* bueno(a)
grandchild *(grancháild)* nieto(a)
granddaughter *(grandóter)* nieta
grandfather *(granfáder)* abuelo
grandmother *(granmáder)* abuela

grandparent *(grandpérent)* abuelo
grandson *(grandsán)* nieto
gray *(gréi)* gris
green *(grin)* verde

H

hair *(jer)* pelo, cabello
handsome *(jánsom)* guapo
happy *(jápi)* feliz, contento(a)
hardworking *(jarduérkin)* trabajador(a)
has *(jas)* tiene
have *(jav)* tengo, tienes, tenemos, tienen
he *(ji)* él
he's *(jis)* él es, él está
healthy *(jélzi)* saludable
heat *(jit)* calor
heavy *(jévi)* pesado(a)
her *(jer)* su (de ella)
his *(jis)* su (de él)
homemaker *(jomméiker)* ama de casa
hot *(jat)* caliente
house *(jáus)* casa
how *(jáu)* cómo
how old *(jáu old)* cuántos años
hundred *(jóndred)* cien, ciento
hunger *(jánguer)* hambre
hungry *(jángri)* hambriento(a)
husband *(jásben)* esposo

I

I *(ái)* yo
I'm *(áim)* yo soy, yo estoy
identification *(aidentifikéishon)* identificación
in *(in)* en
in love *(in lov)* enamorado(a)
initial *(iníshal)* inicial
intelligent *(intélishent)* inteligente
interesting *(íntrestin)* interesante
is *(is)* es, estaá
it *(it)*
it's *(its)*

J, K

jacket *(sháket)* chaqueta
January *(shániueri)* enero
job *(shob)* trabajo
juice *(shus)* jugo
July *(shulái)* julio
June *(shun)* junio

key (*ki*)	llave	**my** (*mái*)	mi, mis
kiss (*kis*)	beso		
kitchen (*kíchen*)	cocina	**N**	
		name (*néim*)	nombre
L		**nephew** (*néfiu*)	sobrino
lady (*léidi*)	dama	**never** (*néver*)	nunca
lamp (*lamp*)	lámpara	**new** (*niú*)	nuevo(a)
large (*larsh*)	grande	**newspaper** (*niúspeiper*)	periódico
last name (*last néim*)	apellido	**next to** (*nex tu*)	al lado de
laundromat (*lóndromat*)	lavandería	**nice** (*náis*)	agradable
lawyer (*lóier*)	abogado(a)	**niece** (*nis*)	sobrina
lazy (*léisi*)	flojo(a), perezoso(a)	**night** (*náit*)	noche
library (*láibreri*)	biblioteca	**night table** (*náit téibl*)	mesita de noche
like (*láik*)	gustar	**nine** (*náin*)	nueve
listen (*lísen*)	escuchar	**nineteen** (*náintin*)	diecinueve
live (*lev*)	vivir	**ninety** (*náinti*)	noventa
living *room* (*lívin rum*)	sala	**no** (*no*)	*no*
lonely (*lóunli*)	solitario, solitaria, solo, sola	**noisy** (*nóisi*)	ruidoso, ruidosa
		not (*not*)	no
love (*lov*)	amor	**notebook** (*nóutbuk*)	cuaderno
luck (*lak*)	suerte	**noun** (*náun*)	sustantivo
lucky (*láki*)	afortunado(a)	**November** (*novémber*)	noviembre
lunch (*lanch*)	almuerzo	**number** (*námber*)	número
		nurse (*ners*)	enfermero(a
M			
make (*méik*)	hacer		
man (*man*)	hombre	**O**	
many (*méni*)	mucho, mucha, muchos, muchas	**occupation** (*okiupéishon*)	trabajo
March (*march*)	marzo	**October** (*octóuber*)	octubre
marital status (*márital státes*)	estado civil	**of** (*of*)	de
		office (*ófis*)	oficina
married (*márid*)	casado(a)	**old** (*old*)	viejo(a)
math (*maz*)	matemática	**on** (*on*)	sobre
May (*méi*)	mayo	**once** (*uáns*)	una vez
meat (*mit*)	carne	**one** (*uán*)	un, uno, una
meeting (*mítin*)	reunión	**one hundred** (*uán jóndred*)	cien, ciento
men (*men*)	hombres		
microwave (*máicroueiv*)	microondas	**only** (*áunli*)	*solo, sola*
middle initial (*midl iníshal*)	la inicial del segundo nombre	**opera** (*ópera*)	ópera
		orange (*óransh*)	naranja, anaranjado
middle name (*midl néim*)	segundo nombre	**other** (*áder*)	otro, otra
		our (*áur*)	nuestro(a)
milk (*milk*)	leche	**oven** (*óven*)	horno
mirror (*mírror*)	espejo		
Monday (*mándei*)	lunes	**P**	
money (*máni*)	dinero	**painter** (*péinter*)	pintor(a)
month (*monz*)	mes	**pants** (*pants*)	pantalones
morning (*mórnin*)	mañana	**parents** (*pérents*)	padres
mother (*máder*)	madre	**park** (*park*)	parque
mother-in-law (*máder in loh*)	suegra	**party** (*párti*)	fiesta
		peach (*pich*)	durazno
move (*muv*)	mudarse	**pen** (*pen*)	bolígrafo
movie (*múvi*)	película		

English Grammar: Step by Step 2

pencil (*pénsil*)	lápiz
people (*pípl*)	personas, gente
person (*pérson*)	persona
pharmacy (*farmasi*)	farmacia
picture (*píc-chur*)	retrato
place (*pléis*)	lugar
play (*pléi*)	jugar
poor (*pu-ur*)	pobre
preposition (*preposíshon*)	preposición
pretty (*príti*)	bonito(a), guapa
problem (*próblem*)	problema
pronoun (*prónaun*)	pronombre
purple (*pérpl*)	morado(a)

Q, R

question (*kuéstion*)	pregunta
quiet (*kuáiet*)	silencioso, silenciosa, callado, callada
read (*rid*)	leer
red (*red*)	rojo(a)
refrigerator (*rifríshereitor*)	refrigerador
relative (*rélativ*)	pariente, familiar
relax (*riláx*)	relajar
rent (*rent*)	alquilar
retired (*ritáird*)	jubilado
rice (*ráis*)	arroz
room (*rum*)	cuarto
roommate (*rúmeit*)	compañero de cuarto
rug (*rag*)	alfombra

S

sad (*sad*)	triste
salesperson (*séilsperson*)	vendedor(a)
Saturday (*sáturdei*)	sábado
school (*skul*)	escuela, colegio
second (*sékond*)	segundo(a)
September (*septémber*)	septiembre
seven (*séven*)	siete
seventeen (*séventin*)	diecisiete
seventy (*séventi*)	setenta
she (*shi*)	ella
she's (*shis*)	ella es, ella está
shirt (*shert*)	camisa
shoes (*shus*)	zapatos
short (*short*)	chaparro(a), bajo(a)
shower (*sháuer*)	ducha
sick (*sik*)	enfermo(a)
single (*singl*)	soltero(a)
sink (*sink*)	fregadero, lavabo
sister (*síster*)	hermana
sister-in-law (*síster in loh*)	cuñada

sit (*sít*)	sentarse
six (*six*)	*seis*
sixteen (*síxtin*)	dieciséis
sixty (*síxti*)	*sesenta*
sleep (*slip*)	dormir, sueño
sleepy (*slípi*)	soñoliento
small (*smol*)	pequeño(a)
soccer (*sóker*)	fútbol
sock (*sok*)	calcetín
sometimes (*samtáims*)	a veces, algunas veces
son (*san*)	hijo
son-in-law (*san in loh*)	yerno
speak (*spik*)	hablar
start (*start*)	empezar
state (*stéit*)	estado
statement (*stéitment*)	afirmación
store (*stor*)	tienda
stove (*stóuv*)	cocina, estufa
straight (*stréit*)	lacio(a)
street (*strit*)	calle
student (*stiúdent*)	estudiante
study (*stádi*)	estudiar
subject (*sóbshekt*)	sujeto
Sunday (*sándei*)	domingo

T

table (*téibl*)	mesa
take (*téik*)	tomar
take a break (*téik e bréik*)	descansar
take a shower (*téik e sháuer*)	ducharse
tall (*tol*)	alto(a)
teacher (*tícher*)	maestro(a)
teeth (*tiz*)	dientes
telephone (*télefon*)	teléfono
television (*televíshon*)	televisión
ten (*ten*)	diez
textbook (*tékstbuk*)	libro de texto
that (*dat*)	ese, esa, eso
the (*de*)	la, lo, las, los
their (*der*)	su (de ellos), su (de ellas), sus (de ellos), sus (de ellas)
there (*der*)	allá, allí
there are (*der is*)	hay
there is (*der ar*)	hay
these (*díis*)	estos, estas
they (*déi*)	ellos, ellas
they're (*deyr*)	ellos son, ellos están, ellas son, ellas están
thin (*zin*)	delgado(a)
thirst (*zerst*)	sed
thirsty (*zérsti*)	sediento(a)

thirteen (*zértin*)	trece	**what time** (*uát-táim*)	a qué hora
thirty (*zérti*)	treinta	**when** (*uén*)	cuándo
this (*dis*)	este, esta, esto	**where** (*uér*)	dónde
those (*dóuz*)	esos, esas	**white** (*uáit*)	blanco(a)
three (*zri*)	tres	**who** (*ju*)	quien, quién
Thursday (*zúrsdei*)	jueves	**why** (*uái*)	por qué
time (*táim*)	tiempo, hora	**wife** (*uáif*)	esposa
tired (*táierd*)	cansado(a)	**window** (*uíndou*)	ventana
to be (*tu bi*)	ser, estar	**woman** (*uéman*)	mujer
today (*tudéi*)	hoy	**women** (*uémen*)	mujeres
toilet (*tóilet*)	excusado	**work (noun)** (*uérk*)	trabajo
tooth (*tuz*)	diente	**work (verb)** (*uérk*)	trabajar
towel (*táuel*)	toalla	**write** (*ráit*)	escribir
toy (*tói*)	juguete	**year** (*íer*)	año
tree (*tri*)	árbol	**yellow** (*iélou*)	amarillo(a)
Tuesday (*tiúsdei*)	martes	**yes** (*iés*)	sí
twelve (*tuélf*)	doce	**you** (*iú*)	tú, usted, ustedes
twenty (*tuénti*)	*veinte*	**you're** (*iúr*)	tú eres, tú estás, usted es, usted está, ustedes, son, ustedes están
twice (*tuáis*)	dos veces		
two (*tu*)	dos		
		young (*iáng*)	joven
		your (*iór*)	tu, tus, su, sus

U, V

		zip code (*tsip cóud*)	código postal
ugly (*ógli*)	feo(a)		
uncle (*oncl*)	tío		
under (*ánder*)	debajo de		
unusual (*aniúshal*)	inusual		
usually (*iúshali*)	normalmente		
vegetables (*véshetabls*)	vegetales		
verb (*verb*)	verbo		
very (*véri*)	muy		
visit (*vísit*)	visitar		
volleyball (*vóleibol*)	voleibol		
vowel (*váuel*)	vocal		

W, X, Y, Z

waiter (*uéiter*)	mesero
waitress (*uéitres*)	mesera
walk (*uók*)	caminar
wall (*uól*)	pared
want (*uánt)*	querer
wash (*uósh*)	lavar
watch (*uách*)	mirar
watermelon (*uátermelon*)	sandía
we (*uí*)	nosotros, nosotras
we're (*uér*)	somos, estamos
wear (*uér*)	usar, llevar puesto
weather (*uéder*)	clima, tiempo
Wednesday (*uénsdei*)	miércoles
weekend (*uíken*)	fin de semana
what (*uát*)	qué, cuál

Spanish/English Dictionary

A

a	at (*at*)
a qué hora	what time (*uát-táim*)
a veces	sometimes (*samtáims*)
abogado(a)	lawyer (*lóier*)
abrigo	coat (*cóut*)
abril	April (*éiprel*)
abuela	grandmother (*granmáder*)
abuelo	grandfather (*granfáder*)
abuelos	grandparents, (*grandpérents*)
acostarse	go to bed (*góu tu bed*)
adjetivo	adjective (*ádshetiv*)
afirmación	statement (*stéitment*)
afortunado(a)	lucky (*láki*)
agosto	August (*ógost*)
agradable	nice (*náis*)
al lado de	next to (*nex tu*)
albañil	construction worker (*constrókshon uérker*)
alfombra	rug (*rag*)
algunas veces	sometimes (*samtáims*)
allí	there (*der*)
almuerzo	lunch (*lanch*)
alquilar	rent (*rent*)
alto(a)	tall (*tol*)
ama de casa	homemaker (*jom-méiker*)
amarillo(a)	yellow (*iélou*)
amigo(a)	friend (*frend*)
amor	love (*lov*)
antes	before (*bifór*)
año	year (*íer*)
apellido	last name (*last néim*)
árbol	tree (*tri*)
arquitecto(a)	architect (*árquetect*)
arreglar,	fix (*fix*)
arriba de	above (*abóv*)
arroz	rice (*ráis*)
artista	artist (*ártist*)
aula,	classroom (*clásrrum*)
avión	airplane (*érplein*)
azul	blue (*blu*)

B

bajo(a)	short (*short*)
bañera	bathtub (*báztab*)
baño	bathroom (*bázrrum*)
barato(a)	cheap (*chip*)
bebé(a)	baby (*béibi*)
beso	kiss (*kis*)
biblioteca	library (*láibreri*)
blanco(a)	white (*uáit*)

blusa	blouse (*bláus*)
bolígrafo	pen (*pen*)
bolsa	bag (*bag*)
bonito(a)	pretty (*príti*), beautiful (*biútiful*)
borrador	eraser (*irréiser*)
bueno(a)	good (*gud*)

C

cabello	hair ((*jer*)
café	coffee (*cófi*), brown (*bráun*)
caja	box (*box*)
cajero(a)	cashier (*cashíer*)
calcetín	sock (*sok*)
caliente	hot (*jat*)
callado(a)	quiet (*kuáiet*)
calle	street (*strit*)
calor	heat (*jit*)
cama	bed (*bed*)
caminar	walk (*uók*)
camisa	shirt (*shert*)
cansado(a)	tired (*táierd*)
cargar	carry (*kérri*)
carne	meat (*mit*)
caro(a)	expensive (*expénsif*)
carpintero	carpenter (*cárpenter*)
carro	car (*car*)
casa	house (*jáus*)
casado(a)	married (*márid*)
castaño	brown (*bráun*)
catorce	fourteen (*fórtin*)
cena	dinner (*díner*)
cepillar	brush (*brash*)
cereza	cherry (*chérri*)
chaparro(a)	short (*short*)
chaqueta	jacket (*sháket*)
chistoso(a)	funny (*fáni*)
cien, ciento	hundred (*jóndred*)
cinco	five (*fáiv*)
cincuenta	fifty (*fífti*)
cita	appointment (*apóintment*)
ciudad	city (*síti*)
clase	class (*clas*)
clase	class (*clas*)
clima	weather (*uéder*)
cocina	kitchen (*kíchen*), stove (*stóuv*)
cocinero(a)	cook (noun) (*cuk*)
código	code (*cóud*)
código de área	area code (*érea cóud*)

código postal	zip code (*tsip cóud*)	dos veces	twice (*tuáis*)
color	color (*cólor*)	ducha	shower (*sháuer*)
comer	eat (*it*)	ducharse	take a shower (*téik e sháuer*)
cómo	how (*jáu*)	durazno	peach (*pich*)
cómoda	dresser (*dréser*)		
compañero de cuarto	roommate (*rúmeit*)		
compañía	company (*cómpani*)	**E**	
completo(a)	complete (*complít*)	edad	age (*éish*)
comprar	buy (*bái*)	el	the (*de*)
computadora	computer (*compiúter*)	él	he (*ji*)
consonante	consonant (*cónsonant*)	ella	she (shi)
contento(a)	happy (*jápi*)	ellas	they (*déi*)
cuaderno	notebook (*nóutbuk*)	ellos	they (*déi*)
cuál	what (*uát*)	empezar	begin (*biguín*), start (*start*)
cuándo	when (*uén*)	empleado	employee (*impló-i*)
cuántos años	how old (*jáu old*)	en	in (*in*)
cuarenta	forty (*fórti*)	enamorado(a)	in love (*in lov*)
cuarto	room (*rum*)	encimera	counter (*cáunter*)
cuatro	four (*for*)	enero	January (*shániueri*)
cumpleaños	birthday (*bérzdei*)	enfermero(a)	nurse (*ners*)
cuñada	sister-in-law (*síster in loh*)	enfermo(a)	sick (*sik*)
cuñado	brother-in-law (*bráder in loh*)	entre	between (*bituín*)
		eres	are (*ar*)
		es	is (*is*)
		esa	that (*dat*)
D		escoba	broom (*brum*)
dama	lady (*léidi*)	escribir	write (*ráit*)
de	from (*from*) of (*of*)	escuchar	listen (*lísen*)
debajo de	under (*ánder*)	escuela	school (*skul*)
delante de	in front of (*in fróntof*)	ese	that (*dat*)
delgado(a)	thin (*zin*)	esos, esas	those (*dóuz*)
desayuno	breakfast (*brékfast*)	espejo	mirror (*mírror*)
descansar	take a break (*téik e* bréik)	esposa	wife (*uáif*)
descanso	break (*bréik*)	esposo	husband (*jásben*)
desde	from (*from*)	esta	this (*dis*)
después	after (*áfter*)	está	is (*is*)
detrás	behind (*biháind*)	estado	state (*stéit*)
día	day (*déi*)	estado civil	marital status (*márital státes*)
diccionario	dictionary (*díkshonari*)		
diciembre	December (*dicémber*)	estamos	are (*ar*)
diecinueve	nineteen (*náintin*)	están	are (*ar*)
dieciocho	eighteen (*éitin*)	estar	to be (*tu bi*)
dieciséis	sixteen (*síxtin*)	estas	these (*díis*)
diecisiete	seventeen (*séventin*)	estás	are (*ar*)
diente	tooth (*tuz*)	este	this (*dis*)
dientes	teeth (*tiz*)	esto	this *dis*)
diez	ten (*ten*)	estos	these (*díis*)
dinero	money (*máni*)	estoy	am (*am*)
dirección	address (*ádres*)	estudiante	student (*stiúdent*)
divorciado(a)	divorced (*divórst*)	estudiar	study (*stádi*)
doce	twelve (*tuélf*)	estufa	stove (*stóuv*)
domingo	Sunday (*sándei*)	excusado	toilet (*tóilet*)
dónde	where (*uér*)		
dormir	*sleep (slip)*		
dos	two (*tu*)		

F

febrero	February (*februéri*)
fecha	date (*déit*)
fecha de nacimiento	date of birth (*déit of berz*)
feliz	happy (*jápi*)
feo(a)	ugly (*ógli*)
fiesta	party (*párti*)
fin de semana	weekend (*uíken*)
flojo(a)	lazy (*léisi*)
fregadero	sink (*sink*)
frío	cold (noun) (*cóuld*)
frío(a)	cold (adj.) (*cóuld*)
fruta	fruit (*frut*)
fútbol	soccer (*sóker*)

G

gato(a)	cat (*cat*)
gente	people (*pípl*)
grande	big (*big*), large (*larsh*)
gris	gray (*gréi*)
guapa	pretty (*príti*)
guapo	handsome (*jánsom*)
gustar	like (*láik*)

H

hablar	speak (*spik*)
hacer	do (*du*), make (*méik*)
hambre	hunger (*jánguer*)
hambriento(a)	hungry (*jángri*)
hay	there is (*der is*), there are (*der ar*)
helado	ice cream (*áis crim*)
hermana	sister (*síster*)
hermano	brother (*bráder*)
hija	daughter (*dóter*)
hijo	son (*san*)
hombre	man (*man*)
hombres	men (*men*)
hora	hour (*áuer*), time (*táim*)
horno	oven (*óven*)
hoy	today (*tudéi*)
huevo	egg (*eg*)

I, J, K

identificación	identification (*aidentifikéishon*)
iglesia	church (*cherch*)
ingeniero(a)	engineer (*inshenír*)
inicial	initial (*iníshal*)
inteligente	intelligent (*intélishent*)
interesante	interesting (*íntrestin*)
inusual	unusual (*aniúshal*)

ir	go (*góu*)
jardín	garden (*gárdn*)
jardinero(a)	gardener (*gárdner*)
jefe(a)	boss (*bos*)
joven	young (*iáng*)
jubilado	retired (*ritáird*)
jueves	Thursday (*zúrsdei*)
jugar	play (*pléi*)
jugo	juice (*shus*)
juguete	toy (*tói*)
julio	July (*shulái*)
junio	June (shun)

L

la	the (*de*)
la inicial del segundo nombre	middle initial (*midl iníshal*)
lacio(a)	straight (*stréit*)
lámpara	lamp (*lamp*)
lápiz	pencil (*pénsil*)
las	the (*de*)
lavabo	sink (*sink*)
lavandería	laundromat (*lóndromat*)
lavar	wash (*uósh*)
leche	milk (*milk*)
leer	read (*rid*)
levantarse	get up (*geráp*)
libro	book (*buk*)
libro de texto	textbook (*tékstbuk*)
licuadora	blender (*blénder*)
limpio(a)	clean (*clin*)
llamar	to call (*tu col*)
llave	key (*ki*)
llevar	carry (*kérri*)
llevar puesto	wear (*uér*)
los	the (*de*)
lugar	place (*pléis*)
lugar de nacimiento	birthplace (*berzpléis*)
lunes	Monday (*mándei*)

M

madre	mother (*máder*)
maestro(a)	teacher (*tícher*)
malo(a)	bad (*bad*)
manzana	apple (*apl*)
mañana	morning (*mórnin*)
marrón	brown (*bráun*)
martes	Tuesday (*tiúsdei*)
marzo	March (*march*)
matemática	math (*maz*)
mayo	May (*méi*)
médico(a)	doctor (*dóctor*)

mejor	better (béter)	ocho	eight (éit)
mes	month (monz)	octubre	October (octóuber)
mesa	table (téibl)	ocupación	occupation (okiupéishon), job (shob)
mesa de café	coffee table (cófi téibl)		
mesera	waitress (uéitres)	ocupado, ocupada	busy (bisi)
mesero	waiter (uéiter)	oficina	office (ófis)
mesita auxiliar	end table (end téibl)	ojo	eye (ái)
mesita de noche	night table (náit téibl)	once	eleven (iléven)
mi	my (mái)	ópera	opera (ópera)
microondas	microwave (máicroueiv)	oscuro(a)	dark (dark)
miedo	fear (fir)	otro(a)	other (áder)
miércoles	Wednesday (uénsdei)	padre	father (fáder)
mirar	watch (uách)	padres	parents (pérents)
mis	my (mái)	país	country (cóntri)
mochila	backpack (bákpak)	pan	bread (bred)
morado	purple (pérpl)	pantalones	pants (pants)
mucho(a), muchos(as)	many (méni)	pared	wall (uól)
		pariente	relative (rélativ)
muebles	furniture (fúrnachur)	parque	park (park)
mujer	woman (uéman)	película	movie (múvi)
mujeres	women (uémen)	pelo	hair (jer)
muy	very (véri)	pelota	ball (bol)
		pequeño(a)	small (smol)
		periódico	newspaper (niúspeiper)
N		perro(a)	dog (dog)
nacimiento	birth (berz)	persona	person (pérson)
naranja	orange (óransh)	personas	people (pípl)
negro(a)	black (blak)	pesado(a)	heavy (jévi)
nieta	grandaughter (grandóter) (grandchild (grancháild)	pie	foot (fut)
		pies	feet (fit)
nieto	grandson (grandsán) grandchild (grancháild)	pintor	painter (péinter)
		piso	floor (flor)
niña	girl (guerl), child (cháild)	playa	beach (bich)
niñera	babysitter (béibisiter)	pobre	poor (pu-ur)
niño	boy (bói), child (cháild)	por qué	why (uái)
no	no (no), not (not)	porque	because (bicós)
noche	night (náit)	pregunta	question (kuéstion)
nombre	name (néim)	preposición	preposition (preposíshon)
nombre completo	complete name (complít néim)	primer(a)(o)	first (ferst)
		primo(a)	cousin (cásin)
normalmente	usually (iúshali)	problema	problem (próblem)
nosotras	we (uí)	pronombre	pronoun (prónaun)
nosotros	we (uí)	puerta	door (dor)
noventa	ninety (náinti)		
novia	girlfriend (guérlfrend)		
noviembre	November (novémber)		
novio	boyfriend (bóifrend)	**Q, R**	
nuera	daughter-in-law (dóter in loh)	qué	what (uát) which (uích)
		querer	want (uánt)
nuestro(a)(os)(as)	our (áur)	queso	cheese (chis)
nueve	nine (náin)	quien, quién	who (ju)
nuevo(a)	new (niú)	quince	fifteen (fíftin)
número	number (námber)	refrigerador	refrigerator (rifríshereitor)
nunca	never (néver)	relajar	relax (riláx)
		reparar	fix (fix)
O, P		resfriado	cold (noun) (cóuld)
ochenta	eighty (éiti)		

retrato	picture (píc-chur)	**sus (de ellas)**	their (der)
reunión	meeting (mítin)	**sustantivo**	noun (náun)
rizado	curly (kérli)		
rojo(a)	red (red)		
ropa	clothes (clóuds)		

T

roto	broken (bróuken)	**también**	also (ólsou)
ruidoso(a)	noisy (nóisi)	**tarde**	afternoon (afternún)
		tarea	homework (jóumurk)
		teléfono	telephone (télefon)

S

sábado	Saturday (sáturdei)	**televisión**	television (televíshon)
sala	living room (lívin rum)	**tener**	have (jav)
sala de clase	classroom (clásrrum)	**terminar**	finish (fínish)
saludable	healthy (jélzi)	**tía**	aunt (jav)
sandía	watermelon (uátermelon)	**tiempo**	weather (uéder), time (táim)
sed	thirst (zérst)		
sediento(a)	thirsty (zérsti)	**tienda**	store (stor)
segundo nombre	middle name (midl néim)	**tiene**	has (jas)
segundo(a)	second (sékond)	**tina**	bathtub (báztab)
seis	six (six)	**tío**	uncle (oncl)
sentarse	sit (sit)	**toalla**	towel (táuel)
sentir	feel (fil)	**tomar**	take (téik)
septiembre	September (septémber)	**trabajador(a)**	hardworking (jarduérkin)
ser	to be (tu bi)	**trabajar**	work (verb) (uérk)
sesenta	sixto (síxti)	**trabajo**	job (shob)
setenta	seventy (séventi)		occupation (okiupéishon) work (uérk)
sí	yes (iés)		
siempre	always (ólweis)	**trece**	thirteen (zértin)
siete	seven (séven)	**treinta**	thirty (zérti)
silencioso(a)	quiet (kuáiet)	**tres**	three (zri)
silla	chair (cher)	**triste**	sad (sad)
sobre	on (on)	**tu**	your (iór)
sobrina	niece (nis)	**tú**	you (iú)
sobrino	nephew (néfiu)	**tus**	your (iór)
sofá	couch (cáuch)		

U, V

solitario(a)	lonely (lóunli)	**un**	a (éi), an (an), one (uán)
solo(a)	lonely (sólo), alone (alóun), only (áunli)	**una**	a (éi), an (an)
		una vez	once (uáns)
soltero(a)	single (singl)	**uno**	one (uán)
sombrero	hat (jat)	**usar**	wear (uér)
somos	are (ar)	**usted**	you (iú)
son	are (ar)	**ustedes**	you (iú)
soñoliento(a)	sleepy (slípi)	**vegetales**	vegetables (véshetabls)
soy	am (am)	**veinte**	twenty (tuénti)
su (de él)	his (jis)	**vendedor(a)**	salesperson (séilsperson)
su (de ella)	her (jer)	**ventana**	window (uíndou)
su (de ellas)	their (der)	**verbo**	verb (verb)
su (de ellos)	their (der)	**verde**	green (grin)
sucio(a)	dirty (dérti)	**vestido**	dress (dres)
suegra	mother-in-law (máder in loh)	**viejo(a)**	old (old)
		viernes	Friday (fráidei)
suegro	father-in-law (fáder in loh)	**visitar**	visit (vísit)
suerte	luck (lak)	**vivir**	live (lev)
sujeto	subject (sóbshekt)		

vocal	vowel *(váuel)*
voleibol	volleyball *(vóleibol)*

W, X, Y, Z

y	and *(and)*
yerno	son-in-law *(san in loh)*
yo	I *(ai)*
zapato	shoe *(shu)*

Join the *Paso a Paso* Community

Thank you for purchasing *Gramática del inglés: Paso a paso* or *English Grammar: Step by Step*. We hope that it has made learning (or teaching) English a little bit easier.

We are always working to improve our existing books and also planning new ones. Here are some of the projects we're working on:

- Activity Guides for teachers who are using our books in their classes

- An audio CD to accompany our grammar books

- Grammar activities based on popular music

We also can tell you about quantity discounts available to organizations that want to purchase multiple copies of our books.

If you're interested in learning about these or other topics, send us your contact information. When you write, let us know if you're a student or a teacher. You can

- Email your contact information to **tenayapress@tenaya.com**

- Complete the form below

Contact information for Tenaya Press

Name _____

Street address _____

City, State, Zip _____

Email address _____

Are you a teacher? If so, where do you teach? _____

Send this form to

Tenaya Press

3481 Janice Way

Palo Alto, CA 94303

Made in the USA
San Bernardino, CA
02 April 2018